T0341612

CORPORATE VICES

VICES

WHAT'S GONE WRONG WITH BUSINESS?

CHARLES COHEN

CAPSTONE

First Published 2002 by

Capstone Publishing Limited (a Wiley company)
8 Newtec Place
Magdalen Road
Oxford
OX4 1RE
United Kingdom
http://www.capstoneideas.com

Library of Congress Cataloging-in-Publication Data
A CIP catalogue record for this book is available from the British Library

ISBN   978-1-84112-435-3

Substantial discounts on bulk quantities of Capstone books are available to corporations, professional associations and other organizations. For details telephone Capstone Publishing on (+44-1865-798623), fax (+44-1865-240941) or e-mail info@wiley-capstone.com

To Suzy, Cecily and Poppy

Contents

Introduction: Making a Killing   1

1   The Wrong Numbers   11

2   Controlling Interest   25

3   Paying for Talent   36

4   Are You Motivated Yet?   48

5   Advertising Advertising   60

6   Shortcuts   71

7   Mis-calculated Risks   82

8   Big IT   94

9   Looking Good   108

10   Better Times   119

Index   131

Foreword

What's gone wrong with business? Alan Greenspan – America's central banker – thinks he has the answer. On the same day that the final proofs for this book arrived on my doorstep, Mr Greenspan laid before Congress a dissertation of his own on the ills of the US economy. Most of the audience rightly slept through the opening ditties on money supply and inflation whilst Mr Greenspan warmed up for the aria: 'It is not that humans have become any more greedy than in generations past', he intoned, 'it is that the avenues to express greed have grown so enormously'. And whose fault might that be? The hand which launched a thousand IPOs reached out to finger the most expensive collars in the room: 'Manifestations of lax corporate governance, in my judgment, are largely a symptom of a failed CEO'.

Sorry Mr Greenspan, but you're wrong on this one. Bad CEOs, corrupt managers and conflicted accountants are not news. Let's be honest: no one was really surprised to find a few top people on the fiddle, nor should they have been. For starters, if we ever had believed there to be only angels in the boardroom, to what purpose is the great corpus of corporate law and regulation accreted over two fraud-filled centuries?

Such finger pointing may be misdirected, but it is also excusable. Enron, after all, took *Fortune* magazine's Most Admired Company award for 'innovation, innovation, innovation', even before anyone had looked carefully at the imagination applied to the firm's balance sheet. We have been cuckolded, and we need to find someone to slap.

Beating up on CEOs and their friends may make us feel better, but it won't (sadly) help business get better. The feeling persists that whatever remedies are found this time around, such horrors could and probably will happen again. That's because it is not the character flaws of senior executives which have brought us to this sorry state, but those of corporations themselves. It is our corporate, not personal, vices which best explain what's gone wrong in business – the humbling of mighty companies which only yesterday boasted blue chip stability, the crushing debts and the suffocating demands of a whirlpool of acquisition, merger and restructuring, the fatigue incurred by one too many big IT projects.

Corporate vices? A management error, an incompetent plan, a money losing practice becomes a corporate vice not upon repetition, but when people in a company just accept it. They shouldn't, of course, but they do. A bad idea highly praised is still a bad idea. Corporate vices are the inconsistencies, vanities and deceptions in which an organization indulges itself, always against its own best business interest, and always with justification. Corporate vices are business mistakes the company rewards.

It's easy to pick on faddish management theories as the fertilizer of bad things made good, so I will. Just as Alan Greenspan sat there on Capitol Hill blaming CEOs for the whole mess, a different side of corporate life was being aired in the *Financial Times* by Lucy Kellaway. Ms Kellaway's services to capitalism are perhaps as considerable, if less recognized, as those of Mr Greenspan. She has an eye for exquisitely bad management, and performs great service weekly by giving it the publicity it so richly deserves.

This particular week, Ms Kellaway wished to bring to our attention an exciting development in the important area of management communication: a seminar to be held under the auspices of the Academy of Management in Denver, Colorado. Attendees were to be shown how to get their message across not with Powerpoint, but counterpoint. Managers are being encouraged to sing at meetings, in order to better express their plans, concepts and analyses to colleagues. The title of the presentation says it all: 'Performing Qualitative Research: Results of Research Presented Through Music'.

If there was still a Soviet Union this would be exactly the sort of thing to send even an ardent free marketer running for the border, pleading to be let in. But despite its entertainment value, this sort of nonsense is just the marginalia. Real life is elsewhere, in the day-to-day, self-inflicted wounds of companies large and small, new and old, high tech or old economy. Their failure is simply to do what they were set up to do: being productive with the best possible combination of their people, their resources, creating wealth in a competitive economy.

I have yet to come across a company which does not have such vices. I have (unwittingly, of course) set up a few flawed organizations myself and, as you will see later in this book, indulged myself at the expense of the business, learning to love my bad ideas with the full support of those around me. Being virtuous in business is never easy, but neither is bankruptcy – something I have so far been able to avoid.

One year ago, I lost my company, my job and my place in the sun when beenz.com was wound down. I had started beenz in London in 1998 with the idea to create a new currency, just for the Internet. On the positive side, we did not go bust, I still have my passport, and we returned millions of dollars to shareholders after the company and its remaining assets were sold. But we had also blown through $70m of venture capital, hired – and then fired – three hundred people, as well as opened – and closed – offices in twelve countries in less than two years. Getting into the *Sunday Times* Rich List was considerably more fun than slipping out of it. At least I didn't get a turd mailed to me by a recently laid off employee; that parcel went to someone in our New York office who was far less deserving of it than I. Beenz.com had corporate vices aplenty. I could fill pages with it, but immodesty forbids it.

So this is not a book about beenz, but because of it. The excuses offered by others in other places for the excesses and idiocies of the late-90s boom, that everyone was doing it, it was crazy times, or that it was a new kind of business with its own new rules, just don't wash with me. A business is a business is a business. The opportunities we have might be new, but the mistakes we make never are.

The antidote to corporate vices is what I call business virtue. Not wishing to be wholly negative – and as a confirmed optimist – the case I am making in this book is that productivity is the first, and last, such virtue. The neglect of productivity in modern corporations has allowed our corporate vices to flourish. Belive me, if there were a better word than productivity to capture my meaning, I'd use it. Suggestions on a postcard please.

Productivity once meant the magic by which a company becomes more than the sum of its parts. When you and I work together, making more than we would alone, we have productivity. It really is that simple.

These days productivity means a lot less, and in several different ways. The word is most often used either as a technical term to do with how fast a machine works, as shorthand for efficient workers, or as a thermometer reading for whole economies. This is a shame, because the original meaning is more valuable than any of these, and deserves to be rescued from behind its academic purdhur.

I've been told that writing a book should get easier as you go along, but that didn't happen here. As work progressed over twelve months, the turkeys whose feathers I have been plucking migrated from the columns of the business pages to front page headlines. When I began, few people outside the scintillating world of energy futures had, for example, heard of Enron, but I have recently seen tourists stop and take photos of Enron's London office. As it is located right behind Buckingham Palace, this kind of Chapter 11 tourism may well take off.

All this happened between here and Chapter 10, so every draft required updating and amending just to keep up with events. I had no idea Fish! plc would be declared insolvent halfway through the chapter detailing their dubious environmental credentials. WorldCom cost me a whole chapter. Marconi's ultimate disappearance was on again, off again, on again. If some of what you are about to read has to be retouched by subsequent events, please accept my apologies. Books are not real time, on demand, but that is surely why we still want to read them.

If you would like to contact me with any comments on this book, please feel free. The official website is at www.corporatevices.com.

London

16 July 2002

Making a Killing

J UST BY CHANCE WHILST ON A TRAIN ONE DAY I found myself talking to a man who used to be a vegetable farmer, but now worked as a buyer of fresh produce for one of Britain's top three supermarket groups.

He told me how he'd had the pleasure of receiving one morning a delegation of marketing people from head office. They wanted his help with a cut-price promotion on cauliflower, one of the world's blandest vegetables and also, by no coincidence, a staple of the British diet.

That's no problem, he told them, we can do this in two months' time when our cauliflowers are in season. But the people from head office said they wanted the promotion to take place in two weeks, not two months. That was what it said in their plan, it was too late to arrange anything else, and he had to stick to it. Which he did, by buying the cauliflowers from Dutch farmers with greenhouses and lots of fertilizer, importing them by the container load, and ultimately selling them one third below the total cost of getting them to the shelves. Many more cauliflowers were sold, the marketing plan was met. For this, he received a bonus.

We all know the feeling. Someone, somewhere in the company has made a decision so mindless, so wilfully dangerous, so clearly stupid, that no good will come of it. And nobody stopped them.

It could have been worse, of course. It could have been your stupid decision. And you couldn't stop even yourself.

Everyone knows you don't have to be Enron, WorldCom, Energis or Marconi for things to go seriously wrong with your business.

This book explains why and how millions have been lost in shares and companies, how so many jobs disappeared and mighty organizations vanished into ever thinner air. Can we rebuild trust in these corporations?

What is needed to give us confidence it won't happen again? How do we stop it happening to us?

THE GOOD AND THE BAD

Business exists to allow us to eat without being farmers, and to dress without being tailors. Business virtue is anything that contributes to a company being productive and making profits honestly. It is business. Without it, there would be no corporations, or much of anything else we value in our lives.

If you want to get technical, business virtue is adherence to the economic principle of productivity. That principle says that you and I are productive if, by working together and dividing the labour between us, we can produce more than we would have by working alone.

If a business can harness this magic and sell what it makes at a profit, it is productive and will survive in the market. If it can become more productive, it will thrive.

So anything which enhances productivity is good for a business, and anything which reduces it is bad. Lose too much productivity, for too long, and the company will collapse.

After productivity, everything else about business and companies is detail. What you make, how you do it, how you sell it and to whom, what effect your business has on others, these are the details. Virtue in business means the pursuit of productivity. As my supermarket buyer found, corporate vices make inefficiency seem wise and losses look commercial. They leave business virtue a dead letter.

This book details many of the most common, most dangerous, and most attractive of these vices. Our corporations are sick, and we have only ourselves to blame. This is good news, though. It means we need only ourselves to cure them. When corporate vices are allowed to, they will kill any business of any size. But they are never irresistible: not if you know how to find, and restore, productivity – business virtue.

CAPITALISM IS THE CORPORATION

As horrible as it may seem, this is not a new problem. Corporations have always had their vices, but rarely have we been so accommodating of them.

Two centuries ago, Adam Smith wrung his hands in *The Wealth of Nations* and warned that cliques of businessmen rarely need an excuse to fix prices between them to the detriment of customers and owners alike. He also thought that professional managers were a bad idea in principle: how could you expect business discipline to be maintained, he fretted, when a man was spending someone else's money? In 1856, Abe Lincoln 'tremble[d] for the safety of my country', not from its enemies, but because 'corporations have been enthroned and an era of corruption in high places will follow'. It isn't easy to find anyone, in fact, who has had nice word to say about corporations and the people who run them – even their friends. 'Capitalism', Keynes commented, 'is the astounding belief that the most wickedest of men will do the most wickedest of things for the greatest good of everyone'.

Feel free to complain all you like, but despite (perhaps, because of) these abiding character flaws, wherever it really works to deliver prosperity and progress, capitalism is the corporation. The preferred way of organizing ourselves to do business, few other economic innovations have proven so resilient or resourceful in negotiating the pits and troughs of human misadventure as the limited liability, joint stock corporation.

How resilient? The company you work for today is most likely founded and organized upon the same principles as the first joint stock enterprises two centuries or so ago. At that time, industrialization and trade had outpaced the old way of owning and managing businesses – whereby the whole enterprise (and often their employees) was owned by one person. The reason the great merchants of Glasgow and New York had such large houses was not for their weekend guests, but to house the people who worked for them. If you wanted someone to work for you, you didn't pay a wage: you provided a bed.

This had some serious limits. Exclusive ownership meant it was impossible to bring in new money, to expand, or to professionalize the running of companies. Being a hotelier as well as an industrialist presented some very obvious difficulties if large mills or factories were to be built. Legal partnerships between more than one owner were possible, but wouldn't get you very far: exactly which half of the factory did Sir Bill own, for example, and how could he realize it without knocking the thing down first?

Corporations solved all these problems, and allowed business practice to keep up with the times. The corporate pioneers of the 18th Century developed a way to separate the ownership of a business from its management, by creating shares and boards of directors. Instead of mill owners running their firms themselves, professionals could be employed to do it for them, schooled in the fine arts of book keeping or engineering by, for example, the newly created school for managers at Wharton, Pennsylvania – granddaddy of the MBA.

Of course, it wasn't perfect. There was resistance to the spread of corporations into business life. It took a ruling of the US Supreme court to recognize the right of corporations to exist as legal persons in law, and even then in New York State corporations remained illegal until the middle of the 19th century. It was competition for investment from other states with more liberal attitudes, particularly Massachusetts, which finally forced New York to change its mind.

Corporations proved unstoppable. In the US and elsewhere, lawmakers turned from resistance to give the most generous support. Limited liability was regularized, for instance, giving investors immunity from the perils of bad debts and criminal behaviour by their appointed management. According to the historian Paul Johnson, by 1919, corporations employed 86% of the American workforce and accounted for 87.7% of output. Britain looked much the same. It was suddenly, and permanently, a corporate world.

ONCE WE WERE KINGS

Fifty years ago, the corporation had its real day in the sun. 1945 to 1973 was a period of unbroken growth and expansion in both the UK and US economies. Total output flew ahead, sometimes 4% or even 6% a year, with low inflation to boot – this despite major wars in Korea and Vietnam and a few scrapes around the Iron Curtain.

The post-WWII sunshine was divinely good for the companies driving this long boom, and it was particularly kind to the people who ran them. The main role of the corporation, to bring efficient organization to commercial production, took on tones of moral purpose and the determination of patriotic duty.

Everyone was so impressed with themselves, we even began to believe that management was more than technique; it was a science. How grand! First Galileo, then Newton, and now Peter Drucker.

In *The Practice of Management*, his 1954 panegyric to the men in the white shirts, the ever wise Professor Drucker declared that 'management will remain a basic and dominant institution perhaps as long as Western civilisation itself survives'. Now that was progress. The corporate way of business was good in every way, indomitable, inexhaustible.

This lasted until the mid-1970s, when the weather changed, and we experienced the first recession since WWII – during which the corporate bubble burst.

IT ALL STOPPED WORKING

Drucker's 1954 eulogy sounds so quaint now, almost naive. Trust, even between the people running companies and their employees, is today a scarce resource. A January 2002 Gallup survey in the US found that 43% believed senior executives at American corporations are only in it for themselves, and damn the rest of us. It helps explain a lot of things, including perhaps the fact that the biggest selling business book of the decade is not a guide to success, but *No Logo*, an anti-corporate diatribe by Naomi Klein. Disappointment sells.

The comfortably corporate world described by Peter Drucker actually began to unravel a long time before the current generation of anti-globalists found voice. You can be quite precise about where the decline began – when it dawned on Americans in the early 1980s that their way of doing things was not, after all, unbeatable. What Krushchev had threatened, the Japanese were about to do.

The once prostrate Japan had, unnoticed, developed a new business culture, entirely its own, utterly devastating in its power. Sleepy US industries, from cars to ships to real estate, found themselves unable or just unwilling to compete. For the first time outside of the normal run of the business cycle, large corporations were collapsing or being acquired by Japanese and other foreign investors. Confidence in America's corporate Olympians was flushed away. And as so often happens, what begins in America came soon to Britain.

Suddenly, what had passed as business virtue was now recast as an unnecessary and dangerous, outdated delusion. One particular movement in corporate thinking represented this upending better than any other. The dissipation of corporate self-worth spurred the great, and entirely self-inflicted, succussion of the 1980s and 1990s known as re-engineering.

Many corporations, desperately seeking a decisive break with the past, embraced this violent theory that companies could purge themselves of their inefficiency by literally starting again. And so came the de-layering, the throwing out of experience for youthful energy, the tidal wave of cash into IT, a boom for consultants, a whole new business culture and set of priorities.

There was no accidental exiling of business virtue from corporate culture in the 1990s. In fact, throwing out the old ways was part of the mission of re-engineering, and a point of honour for the new, tougher, corporate culture which was wanting to emerge. Its high priests, James Champy and Michael Hammer even wrote in *Reengineering the Corporation* (1993) that 'tradition counts for nothing. Reengineering is a new beginning'.

EXTRA BRAVE NEW WORLD

The new corporate ways which emerged from the industrial wreckage of the 1980s and 1990s were articulated best by their progenitors, people like Hammer, Peters and Handy. The modern corporation wasn't going to be hierarchical or hide-bound by tradition. It wasn't sentimental about holding on to loyal employees, or beholden to any past practice, process or way of doing things. Most of all, it wasn't afraid, and it wasn't going to suffer the same indignity of being beaten on its own turf ever again.

It all looked so good, for a while, as the NASDAQ began its perilous ascent in the late 1990s and economic growth reached record levels. A lot of people who should have known better even began talking about the end of the business cycle and never ending growth.

To be fair, the new type of corporation in which many of us now work has a lot to boast about, and boast it does. The brochure sells us the flexibility of flattened structures, motivational option pools, cost-saving outsourced HR, sophisticated customer relationship management and, of course, a website or three. We have information systems today which allow you to participate in a conference whilst sitting on the beach (why?) and phones which can find you in any one of a hundred countries. Business is 24x7, super fast, super efficient.

THE SELF-INTEREST GAP

These new corporate ways have so far proven far less able to inspire our confidence than those which they replaced. The ethical blind spots of companies such as Enron and the dubious, if not illegal, practices of others who sought to deceive investors and cover up failure have caused as big a crisis of trust in corporations as any which took place in the 1980s.

The target is, once again, the senior managers and executives running our major corporations. This time, however, they are accused of putting self-interest ahead of business interest. For the first time, a Gallup poll early in 2002 found that employees are as likely as not to expect their bosses to cheat them at some point. 90% thought that those running US corporations could not be trusted to look out for the interests of their employees and only 18% thought corporations looked out for their share-holders a great deal.

Almost daily since the Enron crisis began to unfold, ever fewer people have been prepared to honour corporations with the benefit of the doubt for honesty and good management. The list of near failures and complete washouts has just grown, taking in many of those once considered the blue chip foundation stones of the economy: Marconi, ITV Digital, BT, Kirch, WorldCom, Marks & Spencer, and NTL. The list goes on.

Some do make it seem worse that it actually is. Never one to miss a chance to be on TV, our legislators have not been slow to condemn, either. But having propped up great financial failures of the past decades, such as the trigger-happy, long term capital management, governments are under pressure again, taking a look at the regulation of company auditing for example – not because it says too much, but because it tells too little.

If all was lost, however, this book would not have been written, nor would you feel any need to read it. Capitalism, and its basic institution, the corporation, have a great talent for survival. Even those who hate them think so: why else would they risk life and limb throwing missiles over barricades in Davos each year?

Most of us possess some residual sense of what is good, and not good, for our business. You do not need to have ever run your own market stall, set up a company, or quit banking for a dot com start-up, to know the difference between a good deal and a bad one, a decent proposition and something quite ridiculous. Wasting money is wasting money.

One of the founding virtues of corporations has always been that people can participate in business without being business people, and take risks without being entrepreneurs. When I said that corporate vices are never irresistible, I meant they can always be resisted by you.

TOP TEN CORPORATE VICES

This book looks in detail at the causes, consequences and possible cures for ten of the most common corporate vices. It is not an exhaustive list of everything that can go wrong in a company, and no one should be encouraged to try to develop one either. It's not possible to do so, for if there are any limits to the human capacity for doing bad things whilst trying to achieve the opposite, no one's found them yet.

Chapter 1 looks at the funny numbers, including their much massaged profits, in which we are now expected to read corporate performance. Most of these so-called fundamentals are anything but. For a real understanding of how a company performs as a business, there's only one number worth having: productivity, of course.

Chapter 2 looks at corporate vices which arise when managers who control companies are tempted to confuse this with the prerogatives of ownership. This is one of the oldest corporate vices, and leads managers to act in their own interests, rather than those of the business. I suggest that those who own the business might want to pay a little more attention.

Chapter 3 addresses our almost universal vice for pandering to expensive executive talent. This vice is new, and tracks the growth of the market in top people. It's not a very efficient trade, though, and corporations often overpay when they get talent in, and are overcharged when it fails. Business virtue suffers before, during and after. The message: to only pay for what you get, be absolutely sure what you want, and why.

Chapter 4 investigates another modern corporate vice, this time for employee motivations. You can easily go too far when finding ways to keep people happy, often to the detriment of your business. Taking away the authority of managers, measuring morale rather than delivery and equating less discipline with more effective work really is the triumph of hope over experience. It may not be fashionable, but more organization and discipline can produce a motivated workforce, and higher productivity.

In Chapter 5 we start to look at what corporations do, rather than what they are. First up is a vice for advertising – perhaps, itself, the best marketed product of all time. The more we spend, the less we get. Corporations have allowed advertising agencies to take too much control of their message. No one should know your business, or your customers, better than you. Take it back.

Chapter 6 deals with a corporate vice for taking shortcuts to growth. Corporations in too much of a hurry can blow their money, not to mention their hard earned productivity, either buying up their competitors, or simply paying their customers to do business with them. Neither shortcut seems to work – nor does the next best option, forming an alliance. Business virtue will help you figure out which shortcuts are worth taking, and which are not.

Chapter 7 looks at the corporate vice for predictions. Since every business decision requires you to take some kind of risk on the future, predictions of any kind are nice to have. However, a vice for predictions tempts companies to take big risks on future outcomes which are too far in the future, or simply too random, to justify the stake. Business virtue recognizes the myopia of prediction, and works to make the company more accommodating of uncertainty, rather than less.

Chapter 8 delves into the murky world of corporate IT, and the vice many companies have for big projects of unproven business value. Taking too much at face value, companies invest in big projects and new systems because they feel the need, without a proper business case to back it up. With insufficient scepticism in the ability of vendors – and their own people – to deliver on time and to budget, many projects end up damaging productivity. A new approach is needed if IT is to serve business virtue, but it requires putting the information back in front of the technology.

In Chapter 9 we examine the growing corporate vice for making your company look like a good citizen, in order to satisfy the often conflicting demands of social, ethical and environmental interests. Corporations which play up to them have many ways of appearing to be good, whilst actually continuing to pursue unproductive ways. Business virtue is the pursuit of efficient use of resources; start there.

Finally, Chapter 10 looks ahead with those corporations hoping that economic recovery will come to their rescue. A corporate vice for over-reacting to changes in the economic weather nearly always leads companies to grow too fast in the good times, and inflict too much damage when times are bad. Nearly always this turns out to be good for management, and not so good for investors or even customers. Keeping an eye on productivity, wherever you are in the cycle, is the only way to stay from temptation.

WHERE ARE ALL THE GRAPHS?

Not being a professional economist or management academic, a certain amount of chutzpah is needed to write a book whose central proposition is that productivity is the basis of a sound enterprise. For one thing, I lack the equipment to draw splendid graphs and lay out complex equations to shore up my argument. Lucky you.

The *Oxford Dictionary of Business* defines productivity as measuring the output of an organization or economy per unit of input (labour, materials, capital, etc.). Economists have a hyphenated notion, total-factor-productivity, which amounts to the same thing.

Any business that wants to put a number on productivity simply needs to calculate the ratio between the sale value of what it produced and the cost of doing it. The costs are everything, including marketing and capital investment: all the money that went out the door. So too with sale value: all the money that came in. Put in as much as possible on both sides and you will come out with something approximating the right answer.

Each chapter refers in some way to a productivity-related issue, something which would directly affect the ratio a company can achieve between what goes in one end and comes out the other. By addressing those issues, one at a time if necessary, you should find, if nothing else, that the productivity problems are themselves much clearer. Numbers will guide you; your business virtue will help you finish the job.

July 2002
London, England

The official website is:
http://www.corporatevices.com

CHAPTER 1

The Wrong Numbers

OHN MAY THINKS HE HAS THE NUMBER OF AMERICA'S TOP COMPANIES, and that number is $100 bn. This, he has calculated, is the gap between what the firms in the NASDAQ 100 told us they made, and how much they actually made in the first nine months of 2001. It is also the difference between being able to understand how well a company is doing, and complete ignorance. Indifference is not an option.

Of all the ways to score a business, profitability has had the field to itself for as long as anyone can probably remember. And why not? Businesses are meant to make money. Relying upon profits to measure success should keep life as simple as it should be, give or take $100 bn.

The problem with profit, though, isn't really the recently exposed voodoo accounting practices which allowed WorldCom, Enron and friends to cook the books, their accountants manufacturing returns with abandon. It's not even that we apparently find it so easy to be duped by so many of them. The problem is that profit without productivity is like lying to the doctor. It always catches up with you in the end. Profit is the wrong number, and productivity the right one to look at if you really want to know how well a company is actually doing as a business.

Compare, for example, the very different fates of two of the world's largest networking equipment companies, Cisco Systems and Marconi. Neither have actually made any money for quite some time, although Cisco is a past master at legally conjuring profits where none actually exist: in 2001, it achieved a monstrous audited loss of $3 bn. Pro-forma earnings announcements during the year actually claimed a profit of $0.7 bn – just enough to beat Wall Street expectations and send Cisco shares up a notch or three.

Nevertheless, using their final numbers for 2001–2, revenue per employee was £410,000 ($500,000) at Cisco. At Marconi, even after many thousands of job cuts, it was £115,000. Guess which company lost over 95% of its shareholder value in the same period and saw its bonds downgraded to junk status? Which is still on the critical list? Productivity at Cisco is more than three times that at Marconi. I know where I'd put my money.

DIRTY BALANCE SHEETS

What's gone wrong with profits? Some of those who accept that pro forma statements are a plague on corporate life also argue, almost convincingly, that it will pass. These are difficult times in the economy, they say. Companies are under so much pressure from volatile stock markets, falling demand and margins squeezed by competition. It's harder than ever, but more important, to turn in good numbers. Surely companies cannot be blamed for taking any legal opportunity to puff up their chests?

It doesn't quite convince. For one thing, it doesn't explain why markets – who surely have nothing to gain by being lied to – continue to let companies get away with it. A better explanation is that, for markets in general, and regulators in particular, getting tough on pro forma earnings is tantamount to admitting that the whole thing is just a legalized racket which has been allowed to get out of control.

This should shock no one. It's hardly a conspiracy in need of an Oliver Stone exposé. The whole business of dirtying your balance sheet in this way is carried out in full public view, mostly. Discovering the great gulf between pro-forma profits and actual audited earnings didn't require John May to plant any hidden cameras or hack his way into secret files. Everything was available for free on the Internet. May, a stock analyst for a US investor service, simply added up the companies' pro forma earnings announcements, which claimed a profit of $19.1bn, and subtracted the $82.3bn loss which appeared on their audited accounts.

There is also no mystery as to how there could be such a gap between the two sets of numbers. Pro forma accounts (it's Latin for perfunctory) are added up any way the company wants, leaving in or taking out anything which doesn't fit with the story they wish to tell. Audited accounts have no such flexibility. They must be presented the way the government tells you, using official accounting rules and principles. Pro forma accounts distort the truth just because they can.

Nor is there any real attempt to actively hoodwink investors into thinking that pro forma earnings are supposed to be as reliable as audited numbers. The statements are issued with more health warnings than a box of Marlboro. Guidance notes longer than the news itself generally advise readers not to pay any attention to what's written, and certainly not to make investment decisions on profits that may turn out to be, well, losses. To further help us turn a blind eye, the press statements usually include some kind of platitude from a spokesperson along the lines that the numbers offer a guide to 'core operating performance', or 'trading results', unencumbered by any annoying 'exceptional' or 'financial' distractions.

All this gets dangerously close to blaming the victim. It's our fault for not paying enough attention. Silly us, trading equities on the basis of pro forma statements, for daring to think that the numbers mean what they say.

On the other hand, why shouldn't we take pro forma statements seriously? They are legally sanctioned, and almost completely unregulated. They generate hours of coverage on TV and CEOs take time out from running the company to explain them to us. Plus, if companies really didn't want you to pay any attention to these numbers, why bother giving them in the first place?

Pro forma statements have contributed much to the declining worth of the bottom line as the prime indicator of corporate performance. There's worse to come, too. Financial regulators have done less than discourage the deception that is pro forma announcements. Aside from a few bitchy remarks, and one or two public displays of disaffection, the most they have come up with in practical terms is that if you're going to cook the books, at least be consistent about it.

The first person to find this out was, appropriately enough, Donald Trump – the man who wrote in his autobiography that he likes to put in phone calls to people when he knows they're not at their desks, so he can leave a message without having to talk to them.

When Donald craftily left off a one-time charge of $81 m while keeping in a one-off income of $17 m in a 1999 pro forma for his casino businesses, the inconsistency cost him an immediate 6% on the share price, less another 11% when the regulator ruled the company had, indeed, practiced to deceive. If, of course, Donald had been consistent in what he was hiding from investors, that would have been no problem at all. His shares, like most others who do this, would probably have gone up.

Never mind. We can still rely on audited accounts to tell us how well companies are doing. Can't we?

THE TRUTH, THE WHOLE TRUTH AND NOTHING

It takes about twenty seconds to register for Motley Fool, one of the new breed of isn't-investing-fun advice and information centres on the Internet. Under the slogan, 'to educate, amuse and enrich', Fool's UK site reassuringly advises that 'reading an annual report is actually very, very, very easy'. It's not clear to whom, though. The recommended method for finding out the simplest thing – like how shares a company has issued ('it's not that difficult') – contains more steps than a Rubik cube solution.

Armed, however, with the authorized data of an annual report, and the clarity of a Motley Fool description, actually determining how much profit, or loss, a company actually made is a simple task. A typical consolidated profit and loss declaration will offer just two numbers – before and after tax. The latter, says the Fool guide, represents 'how much profit is left for shareholders after everyone else has had their slice'. A quick calculation of the profit margin is all you need now. 'Companies with margins of over 15% are usually strong businesses'. Excellent. Couldn't be simpler.

It also couldn't be more naive. One reason the pro forma cookery is tolerated might be that governments, and everyone else, still cling to the common fiction that the profits reported in audited accounts are the terrible truth; that you can really tell how strong a business is by looking at them.

Why do we think audited accounts are any good? Search me.

Those busy boys and girls of Stanford Law School have, for the past six or so years, found time between lectures to maintain a comprehensive database of all lawsuits brought by shareholders against US companies for fiddling their audited results.

At number one in its all-time top ten settlements for companies caught cooking the books, Stanford lists the Cendant corporation. Cendant was created in 1997 by a merger of CUC International and HFS Inc. They are in the consumer credit checking and car parks businesses, amongst other things, operating worldwide.

In April 1998, Cendant discovered that one of CUC's business units had been cooking the books, making up revenues, that kind of thing. An announcement went out one evening, just after the markets had closed for the day. When the markets re-opened, Cendant shares lost nearly half their value. The eventual lawsuit which the collected shareholders filed claimed that Cendant's revenues had been overstated by $100 m in a systematic fraud of their audited accounts. The court agreed, awarding damages against Cendant to a total value of $3.525 bn. (You read it right the first time.)

Unless WorldCom can top it – unlikely, since they went bankrupt – Cendant are likely to stay at the top of the league for some time longer. Even so, most settlements for securities fraud rarely slip under $10 m and can easily be ten times that.

Yet, if the courts hope that their firm decisions are helping to keep corporations honest when it comes to their numbers, they will be sorely disappointed. The number of cases and the size of settlements are still rising. There were 487 such filings in 2001, more than twice as many as in a normal year. 2002 looks like being another bumper crop, even without WorldCom.

Audited and pro forma statements may be wide apart in numbers; they may not be so far apart in credibility. This is bad news for everyone, for it finally deprives us of our preferred measure of corporate performance.

THE BOTTOM LINE: NOT PROFIT ANY MORE

The usual answer to these problems is to ask regulators to look at the accounting rules again: it's not what companies say their profits are, but how they say it. Better rules may help, certainly, but not entirely, and not for long.

For one thing, it's not as if the accounting regulations were deep frozen in the 1930s and are just out of date. The rules are always being tweaked, and there have been plenty of well intentioned efforts at international agreements and common practices. New reform proposals to clean up reporting practices come out of the professional bodies all the time, even when they are not being skewered in the media or the courtrooms. But past reforms haven't prevented the abuses we have today. Why should future regimes have any better chance of success?

Declared profits have never been a reliable scorecard for corporate performance largely because they have always been open to interpretation. Any good corporate accountant will tell you that declared profits can be expensive, while being easily and legally hidden. Consequently, you may have very successful, productive, corporations that report very bad – or no – profits on a regular basis.

At the end of the first year of my first business, at the still tender age of 26, I met with my accountant (an honest fellow) to discuss what to do with the profits. 'How much did we make?' I asked. This was a big deal. My head was going to swell in direct proportion to the money made. Came the response, 'How much do you want to make?'

There are all kinds of devices available to you, should you wish to go down this path. Try the very simple device of setting up shell companies, with nothing in them but your tax liabilities. The Republic of Ireland charges much lower duties on corporate profits than does, say, the UK Customs and Excise next door.

Ireland, by no coincidence, turns out to be a very attractive place for many companies legally to declare their profits; the highest contribution to GDP in the whole of the OECD, as it happens. (Tip: incorporate holding company in Dublin, transfer some IP rights, get a dormitory office and someone to answer your phone. Bingo. But I didn't tell you that.)

No regulatory regime will ever completely sterilize accounting practices, or entirely remove companies' room for interpretation. Nor should it: corporations are complex and business life is too varied for such a straightjacket to be of any use. It would probably be unenforceable anyway. Enron showed just how easy it is to evade complex accounting rules which were designed to fence them in to business practices they did not want to follow. But the executives who practised this deception did not invent creative accounting, the world record for which is still held by Cendant anyway.

Companies, however, still need a way for everyone – including themselves – to measure how they are doing in an objective, agreed and honest way. Profits might have fit the bill, if only we were able to agree how to measure them properly – which we can't.

Whilst companies, accountants and governments continue their occupation of the business TV studios, diligently chewing over the problems of counting profits, the rest of us really need to get on with our lives.

GETTING DOWN TO BUSINESS

If not profits, then what? How can we measure the performance of a company without referring to the money it makes? In the jargon, what are the real fundamentals of business?

There are, perhaps surprisingly, more than a few candidates. Surprising because if something really is, well, fundamental, surely it cannot be a matter of opinion? And if others beg to differ, what does that say about your so-called fundamental?

Here's a simple experiment to find out, involving yourself and a few consenting adults. It's like a book group, but for people who read balance sheets. Give five friends a copy of the same company report to take home. A week later, ask which of the many performance indicators it offers is the most fundamental to the business concerned. Although they are only allowed to choose one, don't be surprised to receive at least six answers, or seven if you happen to have included someone who works in marketing.

Some poor souls may still feel no need to look any further than the balance sheet for their fundamentals. Profit will almost certainly be there, maybe cash flow, stock price, indebtedness, gross to net margins. We already know that these don't quite cut it as genuinely fundamental measures, and why – they are sophisticated numbers, their calculation too easily manipulated to suit particular purposes; not basic enough.

Others like to rely on non-financial measures. They can get all holistic on you and talk about the fundamental importance of customer satisfaction, or brand, or maybe employee retention – anything you can't point a calculator at.

The point of this experiment is to show that we've got no idea what's really first amongst our principles, and worse still, we may never have. People quite naturally tend to favour those fundamentals which relate to what they think is important about a company: translation, those which show how important what they do is for a company. And their objectives may not just be different to their colleagues – they can openly conflict.

Investors, for example, have a valuation perspective and a technique for putting a fair price on a company which is seasoned to taste. Some might favour long term asset value, or cash reserves, as their fundamental statement of business success. Their interests will readily conflict with a CEO whose compensation is linked to short term stock prices and has an interest in spending money to grow revenues, not saving it to accumulate reserves. His performance measure is share price.

A financial director might favour fundamentals which reflect her concern for the reliable flow of money through the organization, and oppose anything which looks like a risk to this stability. A change to pricing strategy recommended by a marketing department that thinks the world revolves around market share, for example, would lower margins while draining reserves – jeopardising the CFO's idea of good management.

Instead of asking people what they think the fundamentals of a business are, we should give them a list of candidates and ask whose fundamentals they are. But then, maybe they don't qualify to be called the fundamentals at all. Perhaps we should call them the relatives, instead.

MODERN PRIMITIVES

There is, however, a group of people whose perspective on the fundamentals seems, for better or worse, to be distinct from most other people's. This is the small group of people who invest their own money in a company that they also run.

Unlike even heavily incentivized executives, who stand merely not to make a pile of cash, entrepreneurs who have funded their own companies stand to actually lose it. Like Dr. Johnson's noose, the threat does tend to concentrate the mind. Owner-operators are unique in the corporate world, caught between the lines of the balance sheet when it comes to judging the health of their company. And one measure above all seems to hold their attention: productivity. Why?

It is not hard to understand why this should be, but worth saying anyway. Their own money is at stake. Should they attend too much to non-financial measures, like brand values, whilst allowing the balance sheet to become dilapidated, they will know it and feel it first.

If, however, they are confused about the fundamental dynamics of their business, they will fail to make good or timely decisions, threatening their investment and their livelihood even further. These dangers are present in every corporation; in an owner-operated business, they are present in one person.

When one person is running the show and putting their own money on the line – no matter how large or small the company is – the firm tends to have the most stringent cost controls you're likely to find. Cost-control, for example, is synonymous with pursuing productivity; it means the most important decisions in the company are, in effect, those that involve signing a company cheque. This is doubly true if it's your own money – which is why anyone with a big enough slice of their own wealth in a company tends to be absolutely obsessive about it.

When Mr Bruce Wasserstein became head of the troubled Lazard merchant bank in early 2002, he bought enough of the company to make him the second largest shareholder after the founding family interest. By any measure, even for a man who once made $650 m in a single deal, this was no side bet.

Cost control had not been high on anyone's list before he arrived, but it soon was. His first priority was to replace expensive under-performing bankers with equally expensive, but higher performing ones with even greater share-based incentives. Same money, better value: higher productivity.

Wasserstein had other ideas for his company too. He simplified the ownership structure of the business so that everyone knew what their contribution was actually worth, drawing a straight line wherever possible between work and output. Mr Wasserstein is not blindly trying to preserve the cash he has put into the business, but to make it work harder. His idea is to get productivity back into Lazard's operation, and nothing else.

Even in the sophisticated world of investment banking, productivity is about as fundamental a measure of the effectiveness of a corporation as you can conceive: it counts the value created for every hour worked (i.e. revenues minus costs). Productivity is not affected by anyone's perspective or special interest within a corporation. If costs rise out of line with sales, productivity will fall: even if the costs were due to marketing expenses or pay rises to workers. When productivity goes negative, so does the balance sheet, and so might the business.

What people like Mr Wasserstein appear to know, and the rest of us may have forgotten, is that productivity is the only true fundamental. Productivity is objective. Opinions do not count with it, strategies which disregard it are fanciful and likely to fail. Next to productivity, everything else is detail. Depending upon how you look at it, this is either very obvious, or very, very smart. The shame is, it isn't both.

BLESSED ARE THE PIN MAKERS

When the laws of economics have not been suspended by equity markets with a grudge against their own investors, companies have always been formed and sustained solely by the productivity gains they are able to achieve in the way that they divide their labour to make best use of their available resources. It is only relatively recently, with more and more companies listing on public exchanges, that we've developed our taste for those exotic performance indicators which, while popular, are of such poor nutritional value for those looking to measure corporate performance.

Go right back to the beginning, and you'll see why. Adam Smith, who introduced the idea of the division of labour in the 18th Century when corporations were just being invented, realized that anyone who did not grasp this basic fact did not deserve to be in business, and probably would not be for long. He even makes the point in the very first line of *The Wealth of Nations*. 'The greatest improvement in the productive powers of labour', he wrote, 'and the greater part of the skill, dexterity and judgement with which it is anywhere directed, or applied, seem to have been the effects of the division of labour'.

In what must be the earliest example of the business case study, Adam Smith opened *The Wealth of Nations* in 1776 with a look at an unnamed company in which ten people worked together making needles by hand, at a time when the product was sold by weight and a well oiled production line of this size could produce about twelve pounds worth a day. Smith doubted that if the ten pin makers had worked all day on their own, rather than organizing together and dividing the labour, they would have produced more than a couple of dozen pins between them. He watched them making several thousand.

The reason productivity matters so much, and reveals everything there is to know about any business, is the same today as it was in 1776: corporations come into existence in the first place for the purpose of magicking up productivity, and for this purpose alone.

That companies exist to further productivity hasn't always been uncontroversial, although heaven knows why. No one has ever found a better answer, and most enquiries have come round to agree with Smith in the end, albeit with the addition of a few new wrinkles.

In 1937, for example, the Nobel prize-winning economist Ronald Coase argued that firms exist because they divide labour more cheaply than the market would: that is, organization favours productivity more than competition does. Coase was particularly interested in how transaction costs are lowered within companies, compared to going outside to get things done.

This is what he means: if you and I both work for IBM, you should be able to get my help on a project much more cheaply than if I worked for a different firm, in which case you would have put the work out to tender and negotiated contracts. Companies are uniquely suited to organizing people so that the whole can be made to produce more than the sum of the parts. Who in their right mind would slave alone in poverty when they could get rich working with others? No wonder we don't respect artists.

Coase's theory of transaction costs is now passed around with the butter at most business schools and is chapter one for economics undergrads. A journalist for the *Financial Times* quoted it to me once, and couldn't even put her finger on where it came from. This may be because it's so obviously true, it's easy to forget that someone had to discover it in the first place.

APPLIED PRODUCTIVITY

No theory is worth much unless you can apply it, particularly if you think you've hit upon a universal truth. So let's do that with productivity.

The patron saint of mass production, the Ford Motor Company hasn't always been good at maintaining productivity levels in its plants. It hasn't done too badly though – they are still in business, and many aren't. One reason Ford is still with us is that it always knows to fix productivity first. It did so not very long ago at one major manufacturing plant at Halewood on Merseyside, UK.

Once derided as the worst car factory in the world, Halewood is now a model of productivity. So bad was this place that at one point the UK government had to bribe its owners with £40 m of taxpayers' money not to close it. Today it produces (profitably) the flagship Jaguar 'Executive' car. The people in the plant say the reversal of their fortunes is due to new ways of working, not new workers. There's the soft stuff we're all familiar with: office walls have been knocked down, trust has been established between workers and managers, blah blah. More to the point, everyone is now held accountable to output and quality, with regular evaluations of organization at every level. Efficient working practices are not only enforced but constantly reviewed and refined by the people doing them. They know that faults are their failure, and no one else's. They've learnt to love the division of labour again, and it works.

Halewood is still making cars because the Ford Motor Corporation rediscovered the importance of productivity to staying in business. Frederick Taylor, the founder of modern management science, may well have had this example in mind when writing of '... a complete mental revolution on the part of the working man engaged in any particular establishment or industry' – except that he wrote this in 1911. Something old, something new.

LARGER NUMBER

Many people in business do not understand productivity – literally. A survey by the research company NOP amongst UK firms recently discovered that 35% thought productivity related solely to the output of workers, while 4% thought it measured output from capital. Everyone else was in-between, including the 25% who hold the exotic point of view that productivity is a measure of customer satisfaction and not an economic or financial number at all. This isn't stupidity, it's just ignorance.

A little education will go a long way. Productivity is not a detail; it's a fundamental – perhaps *the* fundamental. It is business virtue. It is not, really, open to interpretation. It is the ratio between what goes in, and what comes out. It is a simple number, which is better when higher and worrying when lower. Its simplicity is its strength – not an easy thing to assert in a business culture so enamoured with its own ability to find numbers within numbers and think this makes it clever.

VIRTUE, THIS WAY

How, then, to reassert the importance of productivity against the tide of facts of spurious importance?

Pills do come sweeter. The Halewood story contains a warning: even though productivity is in the interest of the business, it may be entirely against the interests of one or more powerful forces in the company. First principles are not known for their popularity. Expect a fight, then, between what's good for the business, and good for some in the company. But who's likely to put up the challenge? Probably, no one.

It's fair to ask, particularly if your company isn't owner-operated, or has a deep pocketed boss like Mr Wasserstein at Lazard. Most companies do not. And even when they do, some owner-operators can prove to be just as inept at keeping their business healthy as any badly directed management team. Look at Robert Maxwell (raided the company pension fund), John De Lorean (dealt cocaine to raise capital), or Alfred Taubman (the convicted price-fixing chairman, and controlling shareholder, of Sotheby's). It was their money, too. Self-interest, it seems, is no bar to bad governance.

Looking around the boardroom table, it is immediately clear that no one person has a direct and exclusive interest in productivity. That's the point, of course. It is the measure of measures – a general indicator of activity in the corporation as a whole. No one can own it; everyone does. The IT director may be able to make just as good a case for a budget increase to promote efficient working as could the marketing director who wants to protect margins by spending more on sales promotion. The shareholders sitting as non-executives may prefer to pay off debts, rather than invest in technology, and consider this a worthwhile efficiency gain. It's not looking good for productivity.

It can be done, though. You might as well start with the company report, even the pro forma accounts. Then everyone can separate fact from fiction.

SELF TEST: VICE OR VIRTUE?

Do you agree or disagree with the following statements?

1   Numbers never lie.
2   The more detail we have about the company, the more we understand our business.
3   Financial data is more telling than operational data.
4   Profitability is the best measure of the company performance.
5   Productivity is an obscure economic term that no one understands and only a consultant would ever use.
6   It's more important to use the company report to puff up morale than to portray the current state of the business.

How did you score?

- If you agreed with all the statements, you must have worked for Enron.
- If you agreed with more than half the statements, you have a bad case of this corporate vice. Reread the chapter and try again.

- If you agreed with half, or less than half, of the statements, there is hope for you. Keep up the good work, and consider acting upon some of the suggestions for business virtue.
- If you agreed with none of the statements, you also should have worked for Enron, and maybe they'd still be here.

CHAPTER 2

Controlling Interest

J ONATHAN BLOOMER KNOWS JUST ABOUT EVERYTHING THERE IS TO KNOW about being nice to the people who own the company for which you are chief executive. As the top man at Prudential, one of the UK's largest financial services companies, he now knows for example, that it isn't good enough to offer to double the company's 'intrinsic value' in the next four years, or to continue to outperform the all-share index by a substantial margin, or even to produce another 'staggering result' for them next year. And he knows this because, despite these gifts of his, the shareholders of Prudential very publicly decided to reject a £4.5m pay package for Mr Bloomer and his boardroom colleagues in May 2002.

Who can blame them? Surveying a total loss in the previous year of half of one billion pounds, his shareholders clearly had a different understanding to their CEO of what constitutes a staggering result. They may also have recalled that the board members had received a 44% pay rise the year before, and look what that bought them. Pro rata, the more they paid Mr Bloomer, the worse the company's results might be. Maybe he should have known better.

Few people in his position actually seem to know better. Managers are most likely to pay attention to their shareholders at two times of the year. The first is when the workers want more money. The second is when they themselves want more money. At all other times, the owners just get in the way and the merit badge usually goes to the management team best able to evade their interference.

There is nothing new about this corporate vice, except the way we balance the interests of owners and managers. Economists call it the agency problem: how to get managers, the agents of the owners, to act in investors', rather than their own, interests. It's fair to say that this problem, first identified over 150 years ago, has never been solved to the satisfaction of anyone – as the current dilemmas over executive share options illustrate.

It's also fair to say, I think, that it's got a lot worse recently, particularly as ownership has dissipated between hands-off institutional investors, and there are shareholders in the boardroom as well as the factory floor. As a result, corporations have developed, at their most senior levels, a vice for control – and no longer act as agents, but as owners. One might also say that this vice is a disregard of – or a failure to identify – the interests of owners altogether. And the more they talk about shareholder value, the more suspicious one should get.

This vice isn't going to be good news for anyone – not employees, who at least have the law on their side; not investors, whose interests are often ignored by gung-ho or just misguided management, or by the managers themselves, who can suddenly find themselves high and dry after failed corporate adventures in the exciting world of big deals alienate not only the investors, but their colleagues too. Business virtue requires that no one confuse executive power for the prerogatives of ownership – no one.

INDUSTRIAL RELATIONS: STRIFE IN PLACE

Need to downsize? Have to cut costs? Depending where you live, most employees have the benefit of some variety of industrial relations legislation and, if they're lucky, a union, to help defend their interests.

As a result, management teams faced with the genuinely painful and sensitive task of depriving people of their livelihoods will always want to claim the business virtue of their actions as standing up for shareholder interest. Of course, to do so suits them both: investors get productivity and a stronger balance sheet; management get to deflect blame and keep their bonus.

A method for maintaining your objectivity would be a nice thing to have for these situations, and some people think they've found a recipe for it. The fashionable idea of the past decade is that companies should be run for the interests of all their stakeholders, who are all the people who have a vested interest in the performance of your corporation. Shareholders, management and employees are always included in the collective. So too, sometimes, are customers, suppliers and partners. Even those whose interests a company's actions may affect have been know to be drawn into the fray: neighbours, communities and even Gaia herself.

So what's the problem with this? Stakeholder worthies demand that you give each interest an equal hearing and try to get the best deal for everyone. This is neither desirable for business, nor fair for the stakeholders themselves. It makes running companies far too much like playing politics, as if we did not have enough of that already. Worse still, it's based on a false assumption, that somehow everyone's interests can be aligned.

Talk of business stakeholders began with the fad-wave of strategic management that washed over the corporate world in the late 1980s and early 1990s. The originators of this new discipline, mainly academics, introduced this new phrase as a handy collective noun to describe the participants in making and implementing strategy. As they will be directly affected by said decision, careers might be on the line. It's fair to say that such people have a stake in it. So far, so good.

Left just so, stakeholding would not have been a big deal. But the idea quickly grew into something altogether more problematic. Wannabe effective strategists were taught that the successful implementation of any plan required sensitivity to, and the compliance of, all the 'stakeholders' in it. This wasn't just the people involved in making or carrying it out any more, but anyone in the organization who could get in the way if they wished. In practice, then, that's almost everyone. Soon, it became difficult to work out who was and wasn't a stakeholder, with the burden of proof being on you to rule yourself out. Not so useful after all.

There's more. The very fertile concept of stakeholding quickly spread from the arena of strategic decision-making to corporate governance in general, where it has been able to become merely malignant. The lead was given by, amongst others, the management academic Michael Porter. In 1992 Porter presented the idea of 'inclusive' corporate governance in a paper to the US government on sustainable competitiveness. In short, companies should be run for all their stakeholders, not just their shareholders. The hope is that, if you try hard enough, you really can please all the people, all the time.

It's a very attractive possibility. Inclusiveness makes everyone feel good about themselves, and it caught on quick. One book on company valuations, written in 1994, suggests that 'even in an increasingly competitive world, winning companies provide benefits for all stakeholders.

There is no evidence of any conflict between shareholders and employees.'[1] Sounds great; tastes terrible.

If this were true, we could all go home a lot earlier that we actually do. The direct stakeholders in any corporation do have, however, often violently conflicting interests – and for good reason. Investors have an interest in getting a return on their capital, which may require companies to perform in ways which impress stock markets but may not be good for, say, employees. Such a company may decide, perhaps, to regain investor confidence by shutting loss-making foreign stores. Sound commercial sense, perhaps, but when the UK retailer Marks & Spencer tried this in 2001, Paris took to the streets. The French government was so incensed that the interests of the firm had put profits for shareholders before jobs for people, it took the company to court.

You have to go a long way to find shareholders and employees on the same side. Indeed, when many of the stakeholders in Enron, Marconi and BT found themselves speaking with one voice, it was because they had all just lost their shirts on the company. Even so, the workers and investors soon found the common enemy: their ex-fellow stakeholder executives who had been able to cash out in good time.

JUST CAPITAL

If you find the punch-up between workers and management unedifying, wait until you see the title fight – between management and major shareholders. Poor industrial relations can cause trouble for companies and damage their prospects. Bad capital relations, those between the principal suppliers of capital and those spending it, can turn companies into dust overnight, and instantly destroy billions of pounds in wealth. Just ask anyone who invested in Marconi, Enron, or any one of a hundred late, unlamented dot coms.

It's fair to ask why capital relations has never had the kind of billing that went to its industrial cousin. The answer is: we forgot. True, governments do pass legislation designed to protect small shareholders. Both Britain and the US, for example, have laws protecting minority shareholders from having their interests trampled underfoot by bulls or bears. The law even provides for them to club together in various ways to force companies to take them seriously. But, with the exception of criminal activity, for those

1 Copeland, T., Koller, T. & Murrin, J. (2000) *Valuation*. John Wiley & Sons Inc.

who own the company and who provided most of its capital, it's basically caveat emptor. And managers worried about local laws can always incorporate somewhere more sensitive to their needs. In the US, managers flock to the state of Delaware; in Europe to the Netherlands: they provide useful protections from smaller investors. When Gucci management wanted to fight off a hostile bid from rival luxury goods firm LVMH in 1999, it used Dutch law to avoid putting the offer to shareholders.

In capitalism, though, ownership is everything. In the beginning, what you owned, you operated. But from the 18th Century, bosses increasingly did not own the companies they managed. So what? When Karl Marx warned of the spectre of communism stalking Europe and De Tocqueville travelled America looking for equality, neither felt the need to make any great distinction between the owner and his loyal agent who ran the company on his behalf. After all, most prisoners have no doubt whose side the jailer is on.

They were wrong. Corporations as we know them today first began to appear after industrialisation and international trade had made it difficult or undesirable for even wealthy individuals to fund businesses alone, or to run them themselves. Too much risk, too much money. A mechanism was needed to divide ownership between a number of people who could provide capital to companies without having to actually manage them. This isn't easy when your business is a factory, or a trade route. It made no sense to say that Josiah owned the left half of the factory and Jeremiah owned the right half, since dividing their interests would mean blowing it up.

So people hit on the idea of issuing paper receipts to represent the proportion of the enterprise owned by each person, rather than actually dividing its physical assets between them. Owning companies became something you did, rather than something you were. Someone else, an employee, could then be appointed by the owners to act as their agent in running the business, freeing them from the onerous task of having to do it themselves. As J.P. Morgan later said, the 'leisure class' was modern capitalism.

Not everyone was happy with this wheeze. Adam Smith thought it definitely a bad thing. The owners of a firm's shares, he believed, 'seldom pretend to understand anything of the business of the company; and when the spirit of faction happens not to prevail amongst them, give themselves no trouble about it, but receive contentedly such half-yearly or yearly dividend as the directors think proper to make them.' Worse still, he considered the directors of such companies to have little reason to behave themselves. '[Being] the managers of other people's money than of their own', he wrote, 'it cannot well be expected that they should watch over it with the same anxious vigilance with which partners in a private company frequently watch over their own ... Negligence and profusion therefore must prevail more or less in the management of such a company'.

Smith was right, but not prophetic: investors developed the means of governance that would allow investors to keep management in check. They began to set up regular meetings of boards of directors who could hire and fire everyone from the chief executive down and approve major spending items. Most boardroom debates are resolved by a show of hands: but they needn't be. On the most contentious issues, shareholders have the last and only say in direct proportion to their ownership of the company. The reality of power was very clear. Money talks.

Don't confuse regulating capital relations with removing the potential for conflict altogether, though. The big investors may supply the cash, but what they lack is the time to watch over it. For institutions like pension funds, it's usually a case of too many investments, too little time. A busy partner in a venture capital company can be sitting on a portfolio with tens of millions in over a dozen companies; more, if you travel to Silicon Valley where the figure can reach a hundred. Sufficient attention to a company can mean as little as completing proxy forms to approve management bonuses at the end of each year.

On the other hand, there are some funds, particularly those whose money comes from small shareholders, who like to refer to themselves as active investors. What this means is they keep one eye open, and don't hesitate to interfere when they don't like what management is up to. Warren Buffett, one of the world's most successful active investors, likes to tell anyone who'll listen that he only invests in businesses he understands. Presumably, he finds it easier this way to provide management with the assistance they need in looking after his money. No wonder so many CEOs talk endlessly about building shareholder value: a kowtow a day may keep the active investors away.

Good capital relations are good for business. The eternal merry-go-round of competing interests has proved, in general, to be in everyone's interests, after all. It has allowed some people – investors – to fund companies at arm's length, so that they can deploy capital to where it generates the best return, and create more wealth. At the same time, it has made the world reasonably safe for professional managers and executives to run companies that they don't own in someone else's interest. Investors can share risk with others, making it possible to fund new companies and innovative ideas. Staid companies where the owners have run out of ideas can bring in new management when the need arises. It's a powerful combination – when it works.

SPINNING OUT OF CONTROL

Investors beware: complex ownership structures almost always favour management at your expense. Why? It's obvious: the more owners a business has, or the more remote they are, the less likely they are to be either motivated or like-minded enough to get in your way. Do managers actively pursue this goal within corporations? You bet they do.

To see it in action, look at how new businesses raise cash. There are several ways for management to approach this problem, so why not choose the method that suits your ambitions? Hang around the venture capital business for long enough, or even read the financial pages, and you will come across the notion of managers having a funding strategy entirely distinct from their business plans.

During the Internet bubble of the late 1990s canny start-ups, whose founders or chief executives came from banking themselves, tended to adopt one of two strategies. Some wanted a small number of large investors. This brought prestige, but also security. They hoped that the commitment of the investor would be greater if a larger proportion of his fund was sunk into their business. If things went wrong, the investor was less likely to walk away. Others took the opposite path, actively seeking as wide an investor base as possible. This brought control, and in particular, more flexibility when it came time to go public. When a small group of investors control a business, they can resist a flotation more easily in favour of, say, a trade sale. However, when things went wrong it was much easier for investors to walk away, and many of these companies went to the wall anyway.

Start-ups are a law unto themselves, however. You might also want to look at how management in established businesses can play the game of capital relations as well. One strategy is to spin out whole new companies by surgically removing them, their assets and their people, from the parent. This can hugely complicate ownership structures. Whereas before spinning-off the parent owns 100% of the company, now it owns less of something else. The spin-off issues its own shares, some of which the parent now owns, and treats as an asset in its books. The rest are usually sold to incoming investors to raise capital or are given to management and employees. These structures can be very murky indeed, and hedged with all kinds of side deals when the separation isn't quite so surgical. When General Motors, for example, spun out EDS, its data processing business, special contracts had to be put in place because the parent accounted for over a third of the new company's revenue.

You won't find many management teams objecting, however, that investors can't draw a straight line between their desks. Increasingly, in fact, management teams are taking the initiative in suggesting which parts of their investors' enterprises should be spun out, and how. Since the beginning of the 1990s, indeed, most spin-outs from US corporations have been for what is euphemistically known as strategic reasons – that is, for a purpose defined by management. Prior to this, the majority had been for financial reasons – as defined by the investors. Guess who really wins?

To see just how much these strategic spin-offs and carve-outs tend to favour the management interest, follow the money. In a strategic spin-off, managers first persuade themselves and then their interested investors that giving the business unit in question a full dose of independence will increase shareholder value. They promise that all kinds of entrepreneurial energies will be unleashed, which will make the spin-out more valuable. Although investors will own less of it (they currently own 100%), their reduced stake will be worth more overall. What's more, given the opaque way the assets are accounted for, that value will be a lot easier to count to: just one number – a share price – will do it.

So everybody should win, but no one wins more than the management. A study by McKinsey, consultants of 15 corporate spin-offs since 1996, calculated that 'on average and irrespective of market capitalization, each company's CEO and senior management team were collectively awarded options worth $8 m to $10 m'. Note the caveat, 'irrespective of market valuation'. Shareholders in the parent may be forgiven for feeling they've been taken for a ride. Worse still, there are plenty of studies which show that half the time, spin-offs and carve-outs actually destroy value.[2]

But nowhere is disappointment for investors more likely than in mergers and acquisitions. In early 2000, the value of these deals reached an all time high of $1.3 trn worldwide. It's hard to understand why, however, when the weight of evidence shows the destructive power these deals have on the purchaser's wealth.

2 Source: McKinsey quarterly.

It's hard to fault the logic of a well-conceived merger or acquisition. By buying or merging with company B, company A gets new revenues, and can save overall costs by efficient integration and economies of scale. The whole should quickly be worth more than the sum of the parts. At least, that's what they teach you in economics class – and business school too, no doubt.

The reality is somewhat different. In February 2002, PepsiCo posted a decline in quarterly profits, despite income having risen – so great were the costs of integrating their $13.4bn purchase, Quaker Oats. This is not unusual – but nor is what happens next. Earnings go into reverse, too. According to one long term US study covering most of the 1990s, 90% of companies suffer a slowdown in revenues within a year of executing a large merger. This is what happens when you take your eye off the ball.

A reasonable question to ask is why investors seem content to allow management out on these corporate shopping sprees when they are as likely ultimately to cost them more than they earn.

Perhaps investors believe it's a risk worth taking, in which case, they're mistaken. Some deals do boost share prices, but not by much, nor for long. The average increase in the week or so after an announcement of an acquisition is a feeble 2.65%. Fail to meet higher expectations of increased earnings, as at least half of all deals do, and the punishment is severe. Even on good days, markets tend to mark down by 15% or more stocks that miss earnings targets by as little as 5%.

Some also believe that frequency helps. The Dutch brewer, Heineken, boosted its share price by 12% a year from 1996, simply through the valuation bumps it received with every new acquisition announcement – and keeping revenues on track to ensure the shares didn't slip again. This is rare enough to be remarkable, though. A CEO with an overactive acquisition gland can just as easily swamp his investors, and company, in bad deals.

Take the bankrupt UK imaging corporation Photobition, for example. Everyone blamed over-acquisition for its demise in 2001, but they should have seen it coming. The management of this company had purchased no less than thirty companies since 1995, and then tried to integrate them. This strategy of buying growth had worked at one level. Financial markets applauded, and the share price was healthy. Photobition's profits rose from under £3m in 1995 to over £20m in 2000. But so did its debts. When the ship sunk, the bank balance was red to the tune of over £11m and cash flow had been strangled by interest charges and the costs of looking after all their new businesses.

REALIGNMENT

Corporate ownership has this habit of being too complicated for its own good, therefore getting wildly out of alignment with corporate control. Recently, with the explosion in mergers and acquisitions, as well as a new vogue for management initiated strategic spin-offs and carve-outs, investors have been on the losing side of most deals. But if this misalignment of ownership and control allows too many deals which fail to create value in the long term – and most don't – everyone loses.

It makes a lot of sense to fix it, to bring ownership and control back into alignment, to restore the balance of the mutual interests of management and investors in getting a healthy return on capital from a productive enterprise. How?

Simplifying ownership structures would be a good start. Some smarter management teams are doing just that, in surprising places. Remember Lazard, the investment bank? When Mr Wasserstein took over there early in 2002, the ownership structure was very much on his mind – not least because he'd just bought such a large stake in the firm.

Lazard's antiquated ownership structure had been described as Byzantine and unworkable, even by friends. By dividing ownership between competing entities, factions of the founding family and management in particular, it seemed almost impossible to effect change. Many people saw it as a direct cause of the firm's decline. Standing next to, say, Goldman Sachs it's not hard to see why. Whilst Goldman's partners voted away their partnerships to allow their own shares to be sold on the public markets, the 150 year old Lazard remained fiercely independent through a complex web of cross holdings, friendly deals and family interests. This may have benefited the family in terms of control – but what they had was worth less and less.

In the UK, another complex ownership structure – this one created by the government – has had a similarly rough time. The terrestrial commercial broadcast network, ITV, is not technically a company. For programmes or adverts to go out nationally requires the prior agreement of the local broadcast monopolies which form the network. The defence for this was diversity – but it no longer works. The ITV network was practically bankrupt by early 2002, brought down by its digital TV strategy, and its ability to lose audience share every season. The message even got through to government in the end: in late 2001, proposals were published to lift the restraints that were preventing ITV simplifying its ownership structure.

But the best move of all might be the simplest. Investors need to pay more attention to the businesses they are funding, and ask harder questions of managers whose proposals to swell revenues rely more often on acquiring other companies than on improving the productivity of their own. Businesses need managers who manage at least as much, if not more, than they deal.

SELF TEST: VICE OR VIRTUE?

Do you agree or disagree with the following statements? Give yourself one point for each one you agree with, and no points for each one you disagree with.

1　Management should always act in the shareholder interest when dealing with employee wage claims and costs.
2　Management and shareholder interests are always aligned.
3　If management wants to do something which shareholders oppose, they can always deal with it through the board.
4　The shareholders may own the business in principle, but management is paid to run it in practice. If they want to run it, let them.
5　Management should be entitled to benefit from the risks they take on shareholders' behalf.
6　If the business loses money, the shareholders should not complain. It was an investment, not a deposit.

How do you score?

- If you agreed with all the statements, is your name P.J. O'Rourke?
- If you agreed with more than half of the statements, you might want to consider never holding stock in a company you work for.
- If you agreed with half, or less than half, the statements, you could be someone worth trusting with an investment.

CHAPTER 3

Paying for Talent

T HERE'S A NEW PHENOMENON in the exciting world of business publishing – the exit interview. Traditionally, of course, these are private conversations between HR departments and departing employees, which go no further than a filing cabinet. Now, however, you can open your copy of the *Financial Times* and see for yourself what really goes on when people leave their employers. Not everyone, of course: just top executives, and preferably those who left under what one might politely term less than ideal circumstances.

Celebrity exit interviews which I have seen in the newspapers recently have included some of the key names in the most famous corporate disasters of recent times. John Mayo, for example, had been CEO designate at Marconi when a botched profits warning in July 2001 led to its near obliteration on the stock market. He took the fall for it, and the cash, plus a three-article deal to tell all to the *FT* wherein we discover that it wasn't his fault at all. There was a board meeting which should have been brought forward – to 6AM – but wasn't 'with no good reason'. Apologies? Forget it. He thinks his only real mistake was not to have resigned earlier. Amen to that.

More recently, Stuart Prebble, who supervised the collapse of ITV Digital, chose to give his exit interview to the *Sunday Telegraph* in a full page spread. Mr Prebble appears slightly more chastened than Mr Mayo, but only just. Blaming yourself for everything doesn't make good copy except in suicide notes, and even Sunday paper editors are unlikely to print without at least some buck passing to make the headlines. Stuart doesn't disappoint. Sky, his major competitor, 'is the scorpion'. Government incompetence deprived 60% of the population of the pleasure of Mr. Prebble's signal, instead of the 70% coverage he'd been assured of. He couldn't go into detail about the piracy which affected his smart cards, allowing people to free ride the signals, because it was *sub judice* in California. The alleged perpetrators of the security breach, which apparently cost ITV Digital over £100 m in lost revenues, are none other than a company owned by Rupert Murdoch, the proprietor of Sky.

We're definitely seeing the start of a trend here, the underlying cause of which is partly the number of senior executives, particularly CEOs, who are finding themselves turfed out of their jobs after a few years, and partly the high public profile many of them have achieved independently of the companies they ran. Whichever way you look at it, the market for talent isn't working very well for anyone.

MARKET FORCES

In a company worked on merit, the guy at the top would naturally be the best person for the job. Cream floats, right? Unfortunately, so does some other stuff. Bad news for corporations who find that hiring a poor performing CEO is a case of buy now, pay later – particularly when they get the bill for removing them.

Prices are high for top people, but that doesn't always mean corporations are overpaying. Why shouldn't a good CEO get rich in the process of ensuring great returns for shareholders – including employees? But corporations have a new vice, grown from their taste in picking the most expensive chocolates from the tray: allowing senior executives to fill their boots in defeat, as well as victory.

Disproportionate – some would say, any – exit and loyalty payments to even the most chronic under-performers look a lot like an insurance racket for failed executives, but it's not the employer who's being protected – or the executive who pays the premium. This is entirely the wrong way round. The business virtue of 'buyer beware' has been suspended in the market for talent. If you think this has happened in your corporation, even at the top, ask yourself how far down it reaches. At what point do people stop saying, if the CEO can get away with it, so could I?

Corporations had got halfway to a virtuous business arrangement by tying executive wealth to shareholder returns, but also halfway back by only adjusting executive rewards upwards. This can't be sustained. You'll know this if you're having trouble hiring for senior posts. Price no longer represents value. No market so distorted will ever function efficiently for both the buyers or the sellers of talent. The right people, at the right price, at any level, may never come along if you don't fix it.

THE TALENT CONTEST

Expensive executives annoy a lot of people in the same way that fluoridation of the drinking water once did. Both might be good for us, but why the hell should we have to like it? Some people are just never happy – particularly when it comes to their health, and other people's money.

For example, in Britain and the US, no newspaper editor has to look long to find someone who will complain about the size of an executive pay increase or bonus during the earnings season when corporations are required to make these figures public.

It's arguable that the creation of an intensively competitive, global market for executive talent has been one of the most significant innovations of corporate life in the past fifty years. It's also gone on largely unnoticed by the outside world, to whom it's just job ads with odd acronyms and people discussing their packages in the dark corners of hotel lobbies. However, any corporation of any size can now access the global pool of talent, both in work and out of it, set a price and negotiate a deal through professional intermediaries with no more difficulty than they can, say, choose a new supplier of headed notepaper.

All sorts of trends are conspiring to ensure that headhunting firms' revenues are likely to continue to outstrip the growth of the wider economy by 100% – as they did in each of the past five years. Demography is squeezing the middle aged, and wealth is making us all more mobile. After the razing of hierarchies in the 1990s, employees are more equal than ever in experience and less loyal than ever to a company. Plus, or perhaps because of this, it's fashionable to hire in rather than to promote.

Talent hasn't always been fashionable, or meant what it does today. Talent is the 21st Century's – or at least, this year's – brand name for promise (as in, 'Smithers shows promise', rather than, 'promise Smithers anything to get him to stay'). That's new; the packaging is ideal for a world rich in MBAs and short of contract length. Previous formulas would no longer work.

Not so long ago, for example, companies on the hunt for talent looked for it in your experience, usually measured by years in service. Being promiscuous in your choice of employers often counted against you because it showed lack of willingness to knuckle down or fit in. Fondness is not an appropriate emotion when you look back: these were the days of unpaid apprenticeships and boorish bosses who considered themselves professors of the university of life, where they regularly lectured from the rostrum marked 'Bar'.

Mind you, it has been worse. Go even further back to the 1950s, when Peter Drucker was extolling the wonders of corporate man: the most prized talent was obedience, since people could expect a lifetime of service in which they would be given the skills and develop the experience they needed. How far we have come. You'll have a tough time looking for a role that requires someone who always does as they're told and has no initiative.

According to the management author Charles Handy, 'talent – the ideas, skills, knowledge and experience that drive an organization – is now recognized as the key attribute of every successful business'. He's right: corporate priorities that call for culture change almost always end up meaning people change. Peter Breen, a senior headhunter at the London office of top people's search-and-selection company, Heidrick and Struggles, says that some of his clients come looking not just for a new CEO, but a new soul. They want, in his words, a 'cleaning out of the Aegean stables' – one task of the mythical Hercules, who had to rid the said horse manure in one day. Hercules didn't use a shovel; he diverted a river through it. Mr Breen, it appears, does this for a living. Judging by the quality of his office furniture, he does it well, too.

The problem is, even with people like Mr Breen on hand, the market for talent is too intense; good people are the hardest things to find, and to keep. In 1997, a landmark study by a group of McKinsey consultants – entitled *The Talent Wars* – concluded that 'companies are about to be engaged in a war for senior executive talent that will remain a defining characteristic of their competitive landscape for decades to come'. Don't forget to buy stock in the next headhunter who finds you a job.

IN THE HEAT OF BATTLE

Prices rise whenever demand exceeds supply. The market for talent is no different, at least on the surface. And a talent war sounds like a good basis for creating an effective market in executive talent – one that matches price to quality in order to match supply to demand. It works for Lexus cars, so why not the people who drive them too?

The demand side is definitely there. To see just how fashionable talent is in corporations, a survey in 2000 by McKinsey asked a sample of senior executives, 'how much more does a high performer generate annually than an average performer?' 67% said that high performers in sales generated more revenue. 40% said that high performers improved productivity in operations roles. We must get ourselves some of that.

By all means, but you're going to have to pay. Just as demand is high, so supply is tight. 75% of senior executives surveyed recently reported that their companies had 'insufficient talent sometimes' or were 'chronically talent-short across the board'. Even the supplies of fresh meat from universities and colleges isn't what it once was: by mid-2000, 30% of their talent pool of fresh meat MBAs were still telling researchers that they would prefer to work in a start-up. Who says youth is wasted on the young?

Steady as she goes?

Having said that prices rise when demand is too high, it's also true that they don't keep going up forever. At some point, buyers should leave the market to look for better value elsewhere, or more suppliers should come in and bid prices down again. That, at least, is the theory. It's a pity that it isn't what's happening here, then.

For one thing, talented people aren't entering the market, they're leaving it. Supply of the best talent is certain to remain tight long enough for you or me to go get that MBA we contemplated a few years back. For starters, much of the available good talent has permanently taken leave of absence from the employment market after being laid off, or has jumped ship to something with more options and soft toys in reception. Having tasted forbidden fruit, or simply unwilling to put tail between legs, many of the dot com exiles have opted to become freewheeling consultants living off, rather than in, corporate life.

On the other hand, buyers are not only staying in the market, they're throwing more cash onto the table to up the stakes. Poker isn't a bad analogy.

By 2000, the last year of growth in the US, CEO wage inflation in the US was running at 18%. A survey in late 2001 by Incomes Data Services found that the basic salaries of FTSE 100 bosses, the UK's top companies, rose by an average of 14.8% that financial year and the value of basic salary, bonuses and benefits rose by 18.3%. They shouldn't have; in practice it meant higher rewards for faltering performance – as shares fell, debts rose and profits became a fond memory. Workers' pay settlements came in at 3–4%.

It's easier to understand executive wage inflations when things go well: the market sets rewards for a job well done. It's less easy to explain why prices keep rising when the good times stop rolling. But they do. Why?

Quality falls, prices rise

You could never sell soup this way. For quite some time, the link has been broken between executive rewards and performance. Never mind that such a link is necessary for the proper functioning of the talent market: from a business point of view, it absolutely sucks. It must strike fear into every manager, struggling to motivate staff who feel underpaid, when their most senior boss, the face of the corporation, the spirit of the business, is apparently rewarded a bonus not for succeeding, but for failing. Worse still, a life-size pay-off for leaving before his time. It isn't jealousy at work; it's business virtue reacting to a corporate vice.

How broken is the market for talent? Very, and everywhere.

In Britain, where moral outrage is a national pastime, much of this knavery makes it to the newspapers and TV. In 2002, for example, the board of the UK financial services company Prudential plc (slogan: 'helping you to help yourself'), got plenty of PR when it helped itself to a 44% pay rise – despite the group turning in a loss of £445 m ($630 m).

But other stories are less well publicized and analysed, perhaps giving the impression that instances such as these are somehow new, or exceptional. The problem is, they're not.

McKinsey published a study in 2001 of the effect, for example, on shareholder returns of hiring a new CEO in ten of the world's largest corporations over the past three years. Only three – Quaker, Nabisco and Campbell Soup – delivered positive returns. Seven, including P&G, Gillette and Allied Domecq, showed negative results. ConAgra Foods' new CEO, appointed in September 1997, had delivered a 33% drop in total shareholder returns by August 2000. Many more CEOs are subjected to the ultimate humiliation: seeing the stock price jump for joy when it is announced they are stepping down to pursue other opportunities.

Don't look for an explanation on the downturn either. The divorce rate between corporations and their CEOs had been on the rise all through the boom years; the business cycle has merely upped the tempo. Between 1995 and 2000, one third of America's largest companies changed their chief executive – mostly on grounds of poor performance. In 2001, there were even more rounds of musical chairs: US CEO sackings in February 2001 alone were 37% up on the year before. In the UK, the average CEO of a FTSE 100 company has just four years in the job.

One person who knows as much as anyone about this game is (the actually very talented) Philip Crawford, a British software executive. Since 1999, he has held top jobs at four large, listed, multinational companies. They include Oracle (head of UK), EDS (head of everything outside the US), InterX (CEO) and now i2 (head of Europe, Middle East and Africa). He believes that an incoming CEO has about ninety days to identify and set in motion the changes which will define his success in the post – should he be able to hold onto it.

The loser takes it all

Markets do not misfire without reason, and this is no exception.

Someone has to benefit from a market malfunctioning – usually, the suppliers or the customers, but rarely both. The market for talent, however, is one of those rare instances where absolutely nothing makes sense, unless you recognize the corporate vices which now provide most of its dynamics. Principal amongst these is the vice of paying under-performers to go away – and keeping the true reason for their departure hidden from the market.

You'd be forgiven for thinking that the first people to complain about CEO churn and the talent wars would be the CEOs themselves, since they're the ones being thrown on and off every time the music stops. It's their share options which may or may not be shredded. And as the upheaval involved is so disruptive on businesses, you'd think that they would welcome any ideas that CEOs or business thinkers have to improve things. No chance.

Far from being bad for CEOs, the volatility of their positions and the strength of the market for their talents is very good news. For one thing, it puts the price up, and keeps it up. The evidence suggests that no matter how badly you performed in your last job, as long as you didn't do anything criminal (and get caught), the chances are that you will be able to get back into the game almost immediately and find yourself another place which will appreciate your not inconsiderable talents.

Almost no poorly performing CEO, for example, is ever actually reported as having been fired. In fact, the reasons for a departure before time are rarely, if ever, even mentioned by either party. I know this, because I've done it – and received it, too. The common practice is to present the outgoing CEO with a cheque, contingent upon his signing what's known as a release – a legal document in which each party promises not to talk ill of the other.

Many people outside of these select circles are confused not just by this, but by the apparent complicity of the firms involved. One prime piece of nonsense is the way CEO sackings are announced. Everyone knows that the phrases 'to spend more time with his family' and 'to pursue other opportunities' mean 'we fired his ass'. Most people, one hopes, suspect that 'by mutual agreement' usually means nothing of the sort, and that wishes for future success are uttered through gritted teeth. Some, such as Jack Nasser, former CEO of Ford, take 'early retirement'. He did so in a year of very bad results for his company. Judge this for yourself. The company insists he wasn't fired. Exactly how retiring Mr Nasser chooses to be will doubtless become clear in the fullness of time.

Obviously, having their tracks covered in gold is in the very best interest of the departed, poorly performing, CEO. It means that nothing is going to be said which will leave a blemish upon their professional reputation – or lower their resale price. They may have taken their family on holiday using the corporate credit card, and then filed it to expenses, but no one will ever know. Mum's the word.

Corporations – or rather, the people at the top of them – can also benefit from this secrecy, even though it clearly has no redeeming business virtues. One reason for secrecy might be personal embarrassment for board members. Never mind that they made a mistake hiring this fool in the first place, most are more likely to fear the amount of money they are contracted to pay the man to leave being discovered. If they admit to actually firing him, the severance deal looks even worse.

The roll call of CEOs who have been handsomely compensated for being ousted grows almost daily – despite shoddy returns to shareholders and even less of a contribution to the business. They include Mr John Mayo, finance director and then CEO of Marconi between 1997 and 2000. During his time at the top, the company's shares fell by 90% and its balance sheet went from a surplus of £2 bn to a debt of £3 bn thanks largely to a spending spree on telecommunications equipment makers, which in 2000 *The Economist* said had turned Marconi into a 'high tech plum'.

To be fair to him (and few have been), no one blames Mr Mayo for the turn in the markets – but they do blame him for the way that the company responded. That is their right, but Mr Mayo remains the only person who believes that the £1 m pay-off he received after been dispatched from his post was justified by the contribution he made to it.

Then there's Sir Peter Bonfield, chief executive of British Telecommunications until January 2002, when he received a golden farewell worth £1.5 m. This was despite leaving behind a company which had lost 70% of its value and, under his leadership, acquired corporate debt of £28 bn. His chairman, Sir Ian Vallance, also left in luxury.

But BT's investors may now have learnt their lesson. Sir Christopher Bland, Vallance's successor – who also seems to be doing the job of CEO in all but name – told *The Economist* on his appointment, 'I quite like businesses that generate cash earnings and have a dividend-paying potential. I'm an old-economy person.'

Board seat embarrassments aside, the other most likely reason that few will pick at a departed CEO is also corporate self-interest. The difficulties of finding a qualified (nay, talented) replacement are hard enough already, without the added problem of a reputation for destroying the careers of incumbents after they have left.

One company that broke ranks in this respect – and paid the price – was the FTSE 100 engineering firm Tomkins. When Jim Nicol was appointed CEO of Tomkins in February 2002, it was the end of an interregnum which had lasted seventeen months. Mr Nicol's predecessor, Greg Hutchings, had resigned in October 2000. The company's chairman, David Newlands, had announced an investigation into darkly hinted 'corporate excess' on the part of this CEO. Although the investigation exonerated Mr Hutchings, it severely damaged all concerned – not least the business, which was effectively leaderless at the turning point of the economic cycle. Mr Nicol was in place less than two months after the case with Mr Hutchings was settled out of court.

It's worth asking, then, what corporations think they have to gain from the dysfunctional way in which they acquire – and acquit – their top talent. At some point the interests of their businesses must dictate getting out of this particular bazaar, or so one would hope.

Corporations have contributed to the weird workings of the market for talent in several ways, but the most obvious is the way in which they pay for talent. In particular, companies want their CEOs to behave like driven entrepreneurs: so they have tried to pay them that way. It hasn't worked.

HALFWAY THERE

It all started with a now famous article in the *Harvard Business Review* in 1990 which suggested that if top executives were paid like bureaucrats, they would inevitably behave like them. The general principle, which almost everyone now accepts as the axiom of effective compensation, is that if you reward in the right way, people will perform in the right way.

So the particular way to pay CEOs to behave like driven entrepreneurs, runs the consensus, is to offer them a chance to fill their boots along with the investors – should they generate a good enough return on the capital. Mostly this has meant doling out share options, and lots of them. For a while, everyone loved this idea. Not only were they worth a lot to the CEOs, but they cost the company very little, since the tax treatment of the granting of such awards in the US and UK at least, was somewhat generous. It meant you could offer to pay someone millions, and have the stock market pay for it.

Even today, share options remain the incentive of choice for CEOs, despite the torrid time companies are having in the public markets and the shaking of big sticks by anguished regulators who have (correctly) identified share options as a tax dodge and accounting fiddle. The doling out of share options will probably remain popular, despite these problems, because corporations still think that, details aside, the principle is sound.

In the 1980s, about 2% of executive pay was accounted for by share options. For US CEOs, it's now about 60%. In the UK it is lower – just 16% – but you can expect it to rise with more deals such as those given to Mr Nicol and other captains of industry, such as Chris Gent of Vodafone whose shareholders presented him with a £9.8 m thank you card in 2001. Mr Gent deserved it: he delivered fantastic returns to shareholders for a long time.

The model for this kind of deal is someone like, say, Philip Green, a British retail entrepreneur of undeniable talent at his business. Mr Green became the UK's fastest billionaire in 2001 by buying the failing BHS clothing chain and turning it rapidly around into profit. 'The business would have been broke if I hadn't bought it', he said. In interviews, Mr Green doesn't talk the airy fairy stuff of strategy and vision; he likes to bore interviewers with his grasp of sales per square foot, and how particular frocks are stitched. When he says that he lives his business, he has the trivia to prove it.

Many companies would like to think that hiring CEOs on large options packages will make them more like Mr Green, but they're wrong. What Mr Green and others – like Mr Wasserstein at Lazard – have in common is not that they own a lot of shares in the company, but that they bought them with their own cash, and are using that money to run their companies. As Mr Green puts it, 'the fundamental difference between me and all those tossers running public companies is that I invest my own money. I stand or fall on my decisions'.

CAVEAT EMPTOR

Business virtue would demand that CEO compensation which allows them to benefit from the upside must also – as it does for Mr Green – have some sanction on the downside. Of course, the way exit payments are set these days, the very opposite is the case.

Part of the problem with finding a sanction for failure is that, unlike Mr Green, CEOs are not actually entrepreneurs, betting their own money on their success. Mr Green may be right, but this isn't much good to anyone but himself and the few very rich entrepreneurs who have that kind of money. Corporations could not and should not be restricted – as they once were – to being run by their owners. That's what capital markets are for.

However, the new emphasis on talent at every level of corporations will be for nothing if the problems at the top cannot be resolved. No company that truly believes in hiring the best, and giving them the best, can be credible if its leader is not. When it is clear that even the CEO can consistently under perform and get away with it, even benefit from it, any canny executive who knows his or her own worth might well wonder quite what they're doing in this place.

If corporations truly want talented CEOs to use their skills with the same effect as, say, Mr Green, they must re-cut their deal in principle, aligning it to business virtue rather than the exercise of any corporate vice.

Not easy, granted. The virtuous corporation may need to learn patience, giving people time to succeed. It may also need to learn – harder still – abstinence, driving a harder bargain in the market for talent. CEOs, on the other hand, cannot be led to expect to win in any scenario. They don't have to mortgage their homes when they take the job, but 'no fault' severance clauses which are invoked when they're fired for not meeting their goals should reflect the interests of those who have put money in – not just those who would like to get money out.

SELF TEST: VICE OR VIRTUE?

To test your virtue (or vice), score one point for each of the statements below that you agree with, and nothing for each you don't agree with.

1   The greater the talent, the higher the price.
2   Developing talent is too risky – it'll just walk off with your investment before giving you a return.
3   Executive motivation requires offering upside, but also protecting their downside.
4   In the war for talent, no price is too high to pay to keep talent away from our competitors.
5   Even if executives have no skin in the game, they can still be relied upon to work in shareholders' best interests.
6   When executives fail, no one benefits by letting this be known.

How did you do?

- If you agreed with all the statements, you must recently have been headhunted. How's your new office?
- If you agreed with more than half the statements, you're probably right: someone is after your job.
- If you agreed with half, or less than half, of the statements, you understand the difference between what the business needs and what the company demands.
- If you agreed with none of the statements, when was the last time you took a pay rise? Some time ago, right?

CHAPTER 4

Are You Motivated Yet?

I T'S HARD TO KNOW WHETHER TO FEEL MORE SORRY FOR MICHAEL DAVIES or for Marks & Spencer, the retailer who employed him for nearly thirty years before he was fired on the grounds of having poor people skills. First hear the whole story, then decide.

Until being ejected from his job in June 2000, Mr Davies was a high-flying senior manager with good form for a corporation whose overall grasp on the market was, by then, tenuous at best. He had even been the manager of its Paris store, and in his last posting to a store in the UK, had produced its best returns for over four years. His prospects should have been excellent, but instead of promoting him for his contribution to the bottom line, he was canned.

Why? In early 2002, Mr Davies won an industrial tribunal against his former employer for unfair dismissal at which the details of his departure were aired in open court. Mr Davies had failed a self-administered psycho-metric test used to measure his 'core skills': these were expected to be not selling more, or good organization, but 'looking after' and 'improving' the people he was responsible for. He was expected to have 'sensitivity' to workers' needs as a core skill. He was expected to be good at communicating to 'ensure understanding' or 'influence change'. Nowhere, it seems, was he measured on his ability to sell more.

As his supervisor put it during the case, this was 'about the future, not the past'. His former employer's future at the time didn't look too clever – declining sales, misfiring marketing and boardroom angst were all taking bites out of revenues and share price. The past, one might speculate, had been about disciplined management which was expected to deliver profitable sales first, and staff sensitivity after that. But this particular company put having a happy ship ahead of running a tight one. They're not alone.

A corporate vice for motivation means pursuing the idea that productivity follows motivation, and not vice versa. Simply organizing people more efficiently will not make for better results if they are not motivated to work properly. No one would dispute that we need more motivation: a mere 13% of all men and 22% of women describe themselves as completely happy at work.[1] This can't be good news for anyone.

Yet, as Mr Davies' case shows, a vice for motivation can easily go too far, and worker motivation can become more important than actual results. This vice is more widespread than you might think. Here's why.

HAPPY GO LUCKY

What's the difference between Asda and Marks & Spencer – two of the UK's largest retailers? Staff motivation – and results. Apparently, 84.5% of Asda staff look forward to coming to work every day – and the company enjoys less than 2% staff turnover. In 2002 these scores helped it achieve the title of Britain's best company to work for in a study hosted by the *Sunday Times*. Good for them.

Sadly, we do not know what percentage of staff take similar pleasure when clocking on at Marks & Spencer (slogan: to be the standard against which all others are measured). Marks didn't make it into the Top 100 of the *Sunday Times* survey this year. Nor do we know what their staff turnover is, a figure shrouded in secrecy – even in the company's annual report, which devotes more space to its triumphs in the cashmere coat business than it does to a review of staff morale. Perhaps there's a hint in this.

One other difference between the two companies has, indeed, been their overall business performance in recent years. They've gone in almost opposite directions. In 1997–8, Marks & Spencer was Europe's most efficient retailer, with the highest return on sales. By mid-2001, it had gone on to experience twelve consecutive quarters of declining sales and was busily closing its foreign stores and paying off departed directors. Asda, on the other hand, had sold itself to Wal-Mart in 1999 and is now the UK's third largest supermarket with sales of £9.7bn in 2001, all on a determined but

---

1 British Household Panel Survey (2001) Institute for Social and Economic Research, University of Essex.

very simple strategy of undercutting rivals by around 15% on just about everything. It even outsells Marks & Spencer now in children's clothes. Knickers may be next.

Asda workers are happy and their business prospers. Marks & Spencer's employees don't appear to be, and their business has suffered mightily. Mere coincidence? It is of more than passing interest whether or not these two facts are related. Marks & Spencer, which is currently undergoing something of a revival, believes they are. Like Asda, and the rest of us, it assumes that a happy worker is a productive one – and is determined to make them so.

EVERYONE SAYS SO

There is enough written evidence to fill a landfill which will support the proposition that worker satisfaction is closely associated with performance. It matters not where you are in the company, either. A survey of senior and midlevel managers by the consultants McKinsey in 2000 found that nearly 60% had worked, at some time, under a bad boss. No one benefited from the experience: 86% reported it had made them want to leave the company. Almost as many felt it deprived them of making a better contribution to the bottom line. It's true further down, too. According to the accountants PriceWaterhouseCoopers, a quarter of all British workers believe that they are more productive when they're feeling motivated.

The biggest study ever conducted along these lines was reported as long ago as 1999 – but was so extensive it really does look like the last word on the subject. It was carried out by the Gallup polling organization, and covered over 100,000 employees in hundreds of business units of two dozen corporations in the US. Its data extended over 25 years. The Gallup work shows, beyond any reasonable doubt, that the connection between motivation and productivity exists. (Don't worry, we'll get unreasonable later.)

In particular, there was a strong correlation between performance of comparable teams in the same company, and the well being of the members of those teams. The higher the concentration of workers satisfied with their jobs in a work unit, the more likely it was that that work unit would appear to be one of the most effective in the company. It was also true in reverse: the less happy the workers in a particular team, the lower down the rankings they would be likely to come. Its statistical conclusion was, basically, that the more motivated the worker, the better the work: and that the manager is the agent of motivation.

THE HARD WORK OF HAPPINESS

This is all very well, but to save it from being mere piety, and to keep us occupied, it's worth looking at how corporations have, in search of motivation, tried to put into practice the commandment to make whoopee at work.

Motivational theory used to be simple: pay more money. Some old school types still hold to the traditional view that (in the words of Barry Gibbons, former CEO of Burger King) 'people are coin operated'. Mr Gibbons believes, and is prepared to argue his case, that there are few motivational issues which cannot be solved by the judicious application of cash to the employee in question. He even has anecdotes to prove it, and we've all been there: asked to do extra work, and compensated only with a nice job title, a pat on the back, or a sermon about the value of extra responsibility. Shortly followed, of course, by a powerful urge to return the next call which comes through from a headhunter.

Unfortunately, there is little hard evidence to support this fairly common sense prejudice that money is a reliable way to motivate people for long enough to make a difference. This is true in either relative or absolute terms. A typical Asda employee starts on £8,833 a year – $12,500 – but is amongst the happiest in Britain. On the other hand, Britain's most excited employees are those turning up each day to work for Microsoft. The average Microsoft employee earns far more than an Asda shop floor assistant, but is also much more likely to leave the company when his or her share options make enough to retire on.

You might also want to look further afield, and get a broader perspective. The average British household today possesses twice the spending power in real terms than it did when Queen Elizabeth ascended to the throne. If money were everything, we'd have nothing to feel sad about. So the problem with Mr Gibbons' point of view is that, money motivates, but more money doesn't always motivate more. Less money may not be so destructive either. At one point in the painful reshaping of my last company, one employee wrote offering to take a pay cut, and said others would do the same, if it would help keep the company in business.

Anyway, money hasn't been the motivational weapon of choice for corporations for some time. Managers, and management styles, have been their first line – for example, Mr Davies of Marks & Spencer whose bosses wanted him out, not because he wasn't selling underwear, but because he wasn't sensitive enough to the needs of his charges. He wasn't good, in the words of the management writer Tom Peters, at turning them on.

Tom Peters isn't as fashionable as he was a decade ago, but this doesn't mean he's gone away. Just ask the poor Mr Davies, or even the happy people greeting you on your way into Asda. For it was Tom Peters who, in 1993, really established the axiom – nay, the corporate vice – that a good manager is one who makes a happy worker, because a happy worker does a better job. The book was *In Search of Excellence*, and it remains today the biggest selling management title of all time, unless you include the Bible. We need to look at it in detail, to understand why we are where we are today.

FROM VIRTUE TO VICE

Tom Peters, and his co-conspirator Robert Waterman, set out to turn a particular business virtue on its head. They even said as much. Productivity was not the result of the division of labour, but of employee motivation. It's not how you organize, it's the spirit in which you work which really matters, they argued.

In *The Wealth of Nations*, written in 1789, Adam Smith clearly didn't give a damn how happy the pin makers were at their little roles as they drew, spun, cut, sharpened and shelved. You can't blame him for this: they ate, didn't they?

With the passing of 200 years, however, Messrs Peters and Waterman believed that they knew better. *In Search of Excellence* was published when business was not good in America and corporations were getting the blame. It had got political too. At the beginning of the 1980s, the US (and, by extension, the UK) had woken up one day to a yawning trade deficit with Japan, until recently the defeated and depleted enemy. Total US imports from Japan in 1982 were 400% greater than in 1972, and 220% higher even than 1976.[2] It hurt.

This was a really big deal. Everyone worried; even the professionally optimistic Massachusetts Institute of Technology formed its first national

2 US Dept. of Commerce.

commission since WWII, 'to address a decline in US industrial performance perceived to be so serious as to threaten the nation's economic future'.[3] On the hit list were a bunch of corporate vices which were associated with what Peters called the 'rationalist' approach: mostly red tape and rules which favoured discipline over flexibility, and efficiency over risk.

According to *In Search of Excellence*, the way to restore business virtue was to root out all of these stupefying corporate vices which had allowed Japanese industry to walk all over us. For example, in discussing the performance of Motorola's TV product line after being taken over by Matsushita, Peters and Waterman describe how 'a handful of Japanese general managers managed to cut the warranty bill from $22 million to $3.5 million … and to reduce personnel turnover from 30 percent a year to 1 percent … Matsushita's success in the United States is a vivid reminder of the likely absence of any "Eastern Magic" underpinning Japan's astounding productivity record.' This was going to be good for business. So you see, this isn't the first book to look at corporate vices and business virtues. I'm standing here on the toes of giants.

It was people, not things, that managers should worry about, Peters argued. Japanese managers had a 'focus on product or people'. Americans didn't; theirs was an 'over reliance on analysis … the tools that would appear to eliminate risk but also, unfortunately, eliminate action'. A bias for action was the hallmark of excellence. As was Peters' ideal of a 'turned on workforce' – the 'extraordinary energy exerted above and beyond the call of duty when the worker (shop floor worker, sales assistant, desk clerk) is given even a modicum of apparent control over his or her destiny'. And there it was. The secret we'd all been waiting for. A good business was the result of a happy, excited workforce – and they got that way by managers standing back.

YES, WE HAVE NO MANAGERS

So here's what happened. From the mid-1980s until today, employee motivation has increasingly come to mean empowering staff at the expense of the authority of their managers. Companies stopped seeing their role as directing employees, but as organising them to be, in the jargon of the day, inner-directed, or self-motivated, within a looser, less authoritarian,

3 Dertouzos *et al.* 1989, p. ix.

organization. Even though this is less than a decade old, it passes today for timeless wisdom. It's not, and I should know.

Corporations have, for example, done everything possible to rid managers of the stigma of authority, even doing away with many management job titles in favour of more conflict-neutral terms like 'team leader', 'convener' or (best of the bunch) 'facilitator'. Even those still called 'manager' are as likely to be found in hyphenated specialist roles as in more authoritative general positions.

Whilst running the technology effort for my last company as CEO and CTO, to my great shame, I indulged in a little bit of fantasy management job titles myself. We created a new post in the main development team for a project manager, which I decided to call the entropy manager. Entropy, as you probably know, is the statistical measure of the level of disorder in a closed system – such as a group of socially dysfunctional, too-clever developers. Since entropy is said to increase naturally over time, my too-cute idea was to hire this guy to control it. After we all went our separate ways, the former entropy manager (who had been out of work for several months) asked me for a reference, and help on his CV. This I was glad to give, and I struck out the offending job title. Two weeks later, he had a good offer on the table.

I was only going with the flow, of course. In general, it remains particularly difficult to play spot-the-boss in technology groups. Authority is now almost always hyphenated. In this process, management job titles have been confined to niches (help desk manager, LAN manager) or simply removed altogether (general managers are now vice presidents). This means that everyone, and by extension no one, is seen to be in charge.

You can't even look at what they get paid as an indicator of seniority. Pay scales have been complicated along with job titles: a LAN manager, who looks after your corporate network, can expect to take home a healthy $75,000 a year. The help desk manager can expect at least 10% less. Compensation used to relate to seniority. But since a LAN manager is never likely to be a help desk manager, or vice versa, why bother with parity? In fact, why bother with managers at all?

Unlucky in love?

If flattening out structures, neutering authority, and empowering workers is so great, why aren't we happier? More to the point, why aren't we better off? Where's the productivity revolution we were promised?

A decade after *In Search of Excellence*, the supposed virtues it put forward are, in practice, descending to the level of corporate vices, and the pursuit of these principles can be bad for your business.

There are several good reasons to doubt the consensus view, however overwhelming it is, that a happy company means good business – particularly if, by following this recipe, we are going to do ourselves harm.

For starters, happiness and productivity are not common bedfellows, whatever anecdotal and survey data may appear to show. Rather than comparing, say, Asda with Marks & Spencer, how about putting it up against, say, Tesco – a much closer rival in the UK supermarket sector? Tesco languishes at 100th in the league table of best companies to work for. It doesn't even appear in the top ten for places where people like turning up at work. It's also significantly more productive as a business.

Asda had sales in 2001 of £9.7bn and employs nearly 117,000 people. Tesco had sales of £18.37bn in the same year, with staff of 196,000. In other words, the average Tesco employee accounts for £93,724 in sales. At Asda, it's £83,000. Tesco workers may not be roller-skating to work every day, but they work better and produce excellent results. Strike one against the notion that happy workers are necessarily more productive.

What about, then, the effect on your business of loosening your structure, empowering workers at the expense of management authority? There is a growing number of examples in which corporations have found that, contrary to the received view, less is not more when managing people. In some places, the division of labour itself is back on the agenda.

Take the well-documented decline in UK heavy manufacturing. No sector may have appeared more ripe for a bit of worker-empowered magic, and none has shown more clearly that it can do without Peters' prescription. A study carried out by the consultants McKinsey, published in 2001, suggests that more organization, not less, might be the way ahead. Their analysis tries to explain the blindingly difficult puzzle of why workers in foreign-owned industrial plants in the UK are 80% more productive than comparable UK-owned plants. The poor performers don't suffer from too much management, but not enough.

The study cites the experience of the Ford Motor Company to support what it says. When it took over the UK car firm, Jaguar, workers were producing cars with an average 246 faults per vehicle. After extensive training, this is down to 88 faults per vehicle. Morale is also up: not through having warmer managers, but better training and monitoring.

Training, by the way, is an increasingly common theme amongst those unhappy with the corporate vice of less management for a happier work-force. The UK government-sponsored corporate training initiative, Investors in People, has helped thousands of companies improve the performance of 750,000 or more people, not by giving them a better manager, but by send-ing them on a training course or three. The results have been dramatic for their productivity, retention and employee satisfaction.

Your happy meal, sir

In the spirit of Tom Peters, upon whose toes we are standing, it would be a fitting gesture to wave him away with our own case study in business virtue. If you haven't read *In Search of Excellence* (shame on you), the joke is that Peters and Waterman wrote it by taking case studies of well-run US corporations and extrapolating general principles from their individual experience. And who says management theory isn't a real science?

The business in question will be the McDonalds Corporation. Here is a company whose experiment with the touchy-feely approach to management not only failed to deliver, but did serious damage to the company performance. Now it is being reversed – and it seems to be working.

McDonalds is, by any measure, a highly successful corporation with a devastatingly simple business idea. By the end of 2001, McDonalds had grown to over 29,000 outlets in over 21 countries. No wonder it attracts so much attention from the enemies of global capitalism (whatever that is). On a business trip I took to Tokyo in 2000, my colleagues and I decided to find 'the' McDonalds for lunch – the taxi knew exactly where to go. Wherever one can take a plane to, there is almost no point in the question, 'Is there a McDonalds?'

From 1995 to 1998, McDonalds built a global business around an iron discipline, seemingly insensitive to the feelings and empowerment of employees, with a singular obsession with quality of service and cleanliness. Empowerment it was not. But that was the point. McDonalds is a details business. Or at least, it was.

So notorious are the apparently soul destroying, mind numbing qualities of its manual unskilled labour that we gave it a word – the McJob – which has now begun to enter our dictionaries. The level of enmity that this corporation has attracted from the world's social critics is on a par with that directed towards the tobacco, oil and nuclear power industries. No corporation appeared more ripe for a bit of user-friendly devolution and 'liberation management'. And so it came to pass.

A new McDonalds CEO, Jack Greenberg, began his stint running the company in 1998 by loosening up. Instead of the centrally controlled iron discipline inherited from his predecessors, he devolved power from the centre and gave more autonomy to local managers and franchisees for everything from marketing plans to menus. Mr Greenberg took completely to heart the Tom Peters ideal of a 'turned on workforce'. Some of the results included, for example, a widening of the product range country by country to suit local tastes.

It only sounds like a good idea. The impact of this new strategy was quickly felt. US market share growth went flat. Customer satisfaction fell to levels comparable with competitors – not good in an industry with thin margins and, let's face it, a commodity product. Performance slipped markedly outside the US, even accounting for external factors such as BSE in the UK and attacks by rioting anti-capitalists here and everywhere else. The experiment with empowerment may have satisfied the personal ambitions of local employees to run things their way, but it was no good for the business.

Mr Greenberg deserves our thanks, for he quickly recognized the error of his ways and switched back to managing his organization the old way. The business virtue of productivity through efficient management came to the fore.

Against the tide in the corporate world at large, which is still in thrall to the Peters-inspired vice of less is more, Mr Greenberg started to hire managers back in. He re-imposed a whole layer of middle management to re-establish control over fractious and independently minded franchisees. And, in an affront to another Peters principle, one of 'simultaneous loose-tight properties' (whatever that means), he reversed the trend of decentralization and reduced the number of divisions in the company by 30% so as to be able to exercise more control hierarchically. One immediate benefit, if not the point of the exercise, was to reassert consistent quality control and to simplify the menu, probably at the expense of some of the more exotic and localized items which crept on to illuminated boards around the globe.

Good thing too. At that lunch in Tokyo, I am pleased to report that I resisted the McChicken Teriyaki. I asked the manager how well it was doing.

Not well, sadly. Most of his Japanese customers avoided it too. If they want Japanese food, he explained, there's plenty of it nearby. Will Greenberg Mk II actually work? Perhaps. But one thing is clear from the experience of the past few years: if you want to make people happy, help them make a good business, not help themselves to it. If this means giving managers back their authority at the expense of being popular, then so be it.

AND BACK TO VIRTUE

So the link between motivation and productivity is not what we think it is. You can, as McDonalds found out, give too much room for motivation – Tom Peters style – and lose the benefits of efficient organization. One reason people get paid to work is that they're doing things, and have to put up with stuff, that they wouldn't otherwise. That's why it's called compensation, right? We seem rather to have lost sight of this somewhere in the rush to make people happy and fulfilled at work.

The bottom line is that, for most of their history, corporations had reflected the business virtue of productivity through efficient organization with a variety of authority structures – hierarchies of employees, managers, executives and directors. It has only been since the mid-1980s that these virtues fell into disrepute as writers such as Tom Peters recommended ditching them in favour of a flatter world and empowered workforce.

Ten years on, it hasn't worked out as expected. Yes, there are data which align output with job satisfaction. Yes, too, the company which has the happiest workers in Britain is a successful business – particularly compared to one which is struggling and whose employees really are being compensated for doing time there. But the data don't say that workers are happy because they have done a good job, or vice versa. And in the league tables, the business which is actually doing the best in Britain is 100 places down the rankings of the nicest place to work.

When you come across examples such as Ford or McDonalds, it becomes clear that the formula that Peters gave us, and which we now take as an axiom of good management, simply doesn't ring the bell any more. Both of these companies have a different equation; a business virtuous one. Productivity, they believe, makes for job satisfaction, which motivates employees to do better, which enhances productivity. And so on, and on, at least until their options vest, and Malibu suddenly looks a good place to be at this time of year.

SELF TEST: VICE OR VIRTUE?

To self test on this chapter, simply award yourself one point for each of the following statements with which you agree, and nothing for those with which you disagree. Then rate your score below.

Do you agree or disagree with the statements:

1   Unpopular managers are mostly ineffective at building teams that get results.
2   The most important skills a manager needs are not technical, but interpersonal – such as communicating well, being a good motivator, etc.
3   Companies have benefited by ensuring a closer relationship between managers and workers based upon trust, mutual respect, and a lowering of barriers of authority.
4   The most successful corporations today are also those with the best record at motivating and keeping their staff at every level.
5   Corporations which put the needs of the business ahead of the needs and views of their employees will ultimately damage morale and hence the productivity of their company.
6   Restoring managers to positions of authority based upon their position alone is a retrograde step which will stifle innovation and introduce brakes on change and progress.

How did you score?

- If you agreed with all the statements above, are you Tom Peters, or have you been to one of his seminars?
- If you agreed with half, or more, of the statements, then you are in danger of being too absorbed in the consensus. Read this chapter again until cured.
- If you agreed with less than half of the statements, you have got a balanced approach, but recognize hopefully that productivity is the end, as the basic business virtue.
- If you agreed with none of the statements, you must be one of the few people in business never to have read anything by Tom Peters.

CHAPTER 5

Advertising Advertising

FRED NADJARIAN HAS EXPERIENCED FIRST HAND the power of advertising – and so he should, as a representative of one of advertising's best, and most recent, customers: the pharmaceuticals industry. In April 2002, as managing director of the drug company Roche in Australia, Mr Nadjarian gave an interview to the *British Medical Journal* about how drugs are marketed. If you added up all the statistics put out by companies like his about the many conditions they offer to treat, he said, 'we all must have about twenty diseases. A lot of these things are blown out of all proportion'.

The statistics which worry Mr Nadjarian do, however, sell his products so don't expect them to improve any time soon. 'The marketing people', he said, 'always beat [hype] these things up'. Of course, Mr Nadjarian. That's their job.

Whose problem is this? Pharmaceutical companies argue, with good reason, that they have a right to advertise, responsibly of course, just as any other company. Advertising, they say, can inform patients and support their right to choose. It's a strong prima-facie case. After all, one cannot easily sustain the alternative; that patients should be denied information about their disease and the drugs they take.

Britain hasn't experienced the drug marketing phenomenon yet, but it may be about to. These arguments in favour of advertising prescription drugs directly to consumer are being rehearsed right now in the corridors of the European Commission and national governments. The pharmaceutical companies want Europe to relax draconian regulations that all but ban any direct communication between them and the consumers of their products. They have a multi-billion dollar advertising itch in need of scratching.

They're not alone. Corporations worldwide have a $130,000,000 vice for advertising which they have pursued with unstinting devotion for most of the last hundred years. With only a handful of bad years since 1900, annual increases between 4% and 6% in gross spending are not unusual. Not war, nor pestilence or even depression will ever get between us and our advertising for very long. Lord only knows why.

Those miserable people who say that advertising isn't working like it used to are only half right; the fact is it really never worked as well as we think it did. Figures from Zenith OptiMedia, a media buying company, show that growth in ad spending is almost never matched by growth in corporate revenues, or even consumer spending. Between 1998 and 2000, as ad spending accelerated, consumer growth slowed. Sometimes, the opposite happens: as ad spending fell in 2001, consumer spending in the US and UK actually rose.

It's a fact that advertising is a game with poor odds, and that we do it because we have no alternative, which is also true. Even direct marketing, supposedly the most reliable way to get results (i.e. sales) from an advertising budget, is proud of a mailer which produces a 5% response rate. Well, yippee. You will stretch your imagination a long way before you locate another form of business spending where a 95% failure rate can be considered a success. But still they come, and more every day, for the last hundred years and doubtless the next, due almost entirely to the persuasive powers of the advertising industry, not over your customers, but theirs. Advertising itself may turn out to be the best advertised product of all time.

So the howls of pain coming from Soho and Park Avenue over the decline in ad spending in this downturn look somewhat *parti pris*. Spending is likely to decline another 2% worldwide in 2002, hardly a cataclysm compared to 1938, when US ad budgets took their worst ever drop of more than 8%. But it means the ad business needs to recover its markets, which means selling itself better. In April 2002, Rance Crain, editor-in-chief of US magazine *Advertising Age*, noted this need to get out and sell, commenting that 'top management is more unconvinced than ever that advertising can make a positive contribution to sales and profits'. Prepare to be sold on advertising again. When your corporation has a vice for advertising, for business virtue just read caveat emptor.

THE PITCH

Five years ago, the US had the same kind of restrictions on pharmaceuticals advertising as Europe. Now they don't, and tens of billions of dollars are spent annually on TV and magazine advertising and direct marketing to US consumers for prescription medicines. The problem is, it doesn't really work – and makes the US experience a salutary lesson in how advertising can sell itself into a corporate market far better than it can sell its clients' products to consumers.

Fairfax Cone, a pioneer of mass marketing, once said that advertising is what you do when you can't go in person. For most of their recent history, tight regulations totally forbad direct-to-consumer marketing in the US (and elsewhere, including Britain, where they still do). Business has been done, almost exclusively, using teams of highly incentivized representatives selling to prescribers in person. The UK-based research company, IMS Health, reckons it takes up to 5000 people in suits to launch a drug blockbuster with sales around $500 m a year.

The economic inefficiencies of selling in this way are eye watering – and provide a large part of the reason why drugs are so expensive in the US and elsewhere. Being a sales representative for a pharmaceuticals firm, for example, is one of the most lucrative sales jobs you can get. Starting salaries for reps in the US can go up to $60,000 plus perks. No wonder a small industry has developed to help candidates land these prime appointments; the *Wall Street Journal* reckons that the median salary for a rep in the US is close on $40,000.

No surprise, then, that the pharmaceutical industry jumped at the chance to advertise when it eventually came. In August 1997, the Food and Drugs Administration issued temporary guidelines to manufacturers which allowed them, for the first time, to tell consumers what their drugs were for. They could advertise, albeit within a very restraining regime. But if advertising – however restrained – could replace even half of the reps on the streets, the economic benefits could be blockbusting in themselves – given that cost of sales can consume half, or even more, of gross revenues.

Many pharmaceutical companies gave the ad agency people a big welcome, and the agencies were happy to return the compliment. They told the pharmaceutical firms that those with the biggest budgets had the chance, in the jargon, to own the market. Entire therapeutic areas (as pharma people call your ailments) could become synonymous with their branded medicine.

It has worked well for the advertising business. 60% of spending goes on TV, a fertile space for agencies who do well at each end of the deal. Total spending went from zero to one billion dollars in less than two years. Today, the total is twice that again. By the end of 2001, the top ten US advertising agencies specializing in the healthcare sector billed a total of just under $9300 m between them, according to Advertising Age's Agency Income Report 2002. Growth looks like being maintained as high as 30% a year.

There can be no doubting, then, the success of the advertising industry in selling its services to the pharmaceutical companies. The business results of this orgy of expense are unclear, you will not be surprised to hear.

There have been some successes. 70% of the budget for pushing Claritin, an allergy treatment from Schering-Plough, has been sunk into advertising in recent years. The campaign was so blanket, that even the not-so-sharp candidate Gore singled out Claritin in the US Presidential campaign debates as an over-advertised product. Maybe so, but it worked for Schering: Claritin is now the largest selling medication in its area in the US. Now, with the patent on Claritin due to expire at the end of 2002, the company is putting big bucks into selling the (patent protected) successor product, Clarinex.

But the success of Claritin is rare. In many other product lines, the effect of consumer advertising has been less, not more sales – and greater resistance from the actual purchasers of medicines, the prescribing doctors.

Early on in the pharmaceutical companys' experiment with drug advertising, many prescribers came out in a rash when companies switched promotional spend from them to the patient. Petulance perhaps, but they had a point. Exactly when did reading an advert in *Cosmo* make you more of an expert in correct prescription than several years at medical school? Doctors could reasonably argue that a little knowledge really is a dangerous thing when patients insist on a medication which is unsuitable. Worse still, as Roche's Mr Nadjarian hinted, they may turn up at the surgery thinking they have something they don't – all due to an ad they read in *GQ*.

Some drug advertising did, indeed, have this problem – with bad effects all round. It is widely whispered in the industry, for example, that in 1998 and 1999, Bristol-Myers Squibb spent large sums advertising Pravachol, an anti-cholesterol treatment, direct to consumers – but not to prescribers. This campaign was great in one respect: it significantly increased awareness of the therapeutic area around cholesterol, which grew the whole market, with ever more patients speaking to their doctors about cholesterol problems. Sadly, it didn't do much for sales of Pravachol. The opposite, in fact.

The doctors, neglected by Bristol-Myers Squibb, and no doubt annoyed by know-it-all patients demanding the advertised product, prescribed Lipitor instead, a competitor to Pravachol. And why not? If the Bristol-Myers Squibb rep don't come round no more, what's a poor doctor supposed to do? A year or so later, all advertising spend on Pravachol was dropped, and Bristol-Myers Squibb went back to selling their stuff to doctors, face to face.

About half of all drugs have had their direct-to-consumer advertising budgets cut after the first year of promotion, and the US Department of Labour foresees future growth in the numbers of sales representatives employed by pharmaceutical companies in America – another 75,000 by 2010. It's not likely to be because they expect everyone to be that much sicker a decade from now; it's just that advertising hasn't worked.

Not that this will stop them trying. Barring legislative accidents, there's no reason why their corporate vice for advertising won't grow at the same rate as everyone else's. For one thing, Claritin is not alone in losing its patent this year: according to Lehman Brothers research, thirteen drugs with annual sales of $10 bn lost their protection from generic competitors in 2002. That means a lot of new products have to be sold. It's quicker, of course, to buy TV slots than it is to find sales reps.

Selling out

Most of us would kill to have a product which sells as well as advertising. Maybe you can. There's no secret sauce. Everything you need to know is out on the counter. Take the way advertising is purchased by corporations, through what is best described as the agency system.

It's no surprise that the pharmaceutical companies' first instinct was to take a walk down Park Avenue to find their advertising creativity, strategy and execution. It wasn't because they were new to advertising – the advertisers were new to pharmaceuticals, too – but because that's just what everyone does. Advertising means hiring an agency, not taking on talent.

Corporate marketers have been brought up to instinctively favour the use of outside experts in the creation and execution of every stage of their advertising plans. They will hire in people who specialize in branding, creativity, copywriting, strategy, and casting – and rely entirely upon their professional judgement as advertising specialists to deliver a campaign which works. It's comfortable both ways if things go bad: the agency is paid, regardless of success. The client can pass the blame, and get another agency. If things go well, everyone can take the credit, and get paid. So what's wrong with that?

Tony Manwaring, a UK-based former senior advertising executive – now consulting on his own account – has argued strongly that whilst this might be fine for the technical delivery of a campaign, like holding the camera and puffing the actors, it shouldn't do for the creation of said concept. After all, if you have to bring in a complete stranger to tell you how best to talk to your customers, quite what are you doing holding down that marketing job?

With his insider experience, Manwaring goes further. The consequences of this division of labour, he says, are bad for everyone in ways they simply don't understand. Some of the consequences of using independent advertising services are common to any outsourcing, like budget overruns and late delivery. The advertising industry hasn't helped itself by gaining a reputation for enjoying it, though. The late Jay Chiat, one of many described as a legend of the industry, once commented with some glee, 'we had an unlimited budget and we exceeded it'. This is no way to win friends so that you can influence people, is it?

But the problem specific to the agency system, according to Manwaring, is that the agency system produces beautiful ads, inefficiently. Look at the way the process works, for example, when a TV ad is being put together. First the client gives a brief about the product to be promoted. The agency comes up with a script, which they discuss with the client, research, shoot, research again, re-edit, put on TV. The client delegates creative responsibility once the brief is written; having hired in a creative specialist they have given up the right to any real veto. Worse still, corporations who use this system find that bad campaigns are hard to stop once the commissioning button has been pushed. The agency buys airtime and books media. The timescales mean that substantial changes are rarely, if ever, possible.

The agency system means that clients very quickly lose control to their appointed communicators, and simply have to hope for the best – or at least, wait for the contract to expire and they can pitch out to another agency. However, most corporations with a vice for advertising aren't likely to think so. Maybe they should.

Corporations looking to hire a new agency after the last one failed, or went stale, have no good reason to expect a better result next time round. If they're looking for better understanding of business, and more rounded experience, they will almost certainly be disappointed. Advertising companies in the UK, for example, are staffed by very young people with little knowledge of any business area outside their own. According to the industry's professional body, the IPA, nearly half of those employed by agencies are under thirty. Worse still, if you're looking for an agency to have its finger on the pulse of the mass market, you may be just as disappointed: you may like to know that only 7% of adverts broadcast in the UK are written by women, according to Peter Souter, a senior executive of a large British agency.

The solution is obvious – take back the creative control into your own company. If you want a TV ad, hire a TV producer and camera crew. Advertisers should have no trouble finding talented people with whom to build a good, in-house, creative team which understands and is intimately connected to their business: advertising agencies have shed around 10% of their staff since 2000 as their revenues have declined. Get 'em while stocks last.

Selling what can't be bought

If the way that advertising is sold to corporations helps to keep the market buoyant, it is nothing compared to the creativity of the advertising industry in finding new things – as any good business should – to sell to its clients.

One such innovation that's done a brisk trade in the last decade is the idea of corporate branding, which has been sold to corporations worldwide and spun many hundreds of millions of additional dollars into ad agency revenues. Corporate, not product, branding mind. Product branding, the kind of thing which gets people like Naomi Klein into a lather, at least has the business virtue of being about selling products. Corporate branding suffers no such handicap. It's a way to get your corporation to spend money advertising something you do not sell: your opinion of yourself.

Corporations, like people, enjoy talking about themselves. And like people, they forget that others are never as fascinated by them as they are themselves. Hands up if you think this makes corporate branding a good use of your shareholder's money.

Some, at least, have a shred of an excuse. In January 2001, the world's second biggest drugs maker, British based Glaxo SmithKline, unveiled a new corporate identity, designed for it by Futurebrand, which looks like a guitar plectrum and neatly avoids the pitfalls of having a name with too many consonants by just using the initials GSK. It could have been worse. A year before, GSK had been formed by a merger between Glaxo Wellcome and SmithKline Beecham.

A fondness for initials and obscurities (such as Aventis) is common to the pharmaceutical industry, not just because of its tendency to consolidation, but because it doesn't like being talked about. When public attention does focus on these companies, it's rarely good: a group recently got together to sue the South African government in its own courtroom to protect patents on AIDS drugs.

Ad agencies with clients in need of a spit and polish can do a very good job. They can point to the success they have had with that other corporate leper, the oil business, to show how it's done. A nice friendly rebranding, such as that offered to BP which is now a flower rather than a shield, is just the start. Add a few environmentally sound noises, a long ad campaign, and before you know it, the protestors aren't picketing your refineries or disrupting your AGM.

But protecting your good name, or even spelling it correctly, cannot justify the great sums and grandiose campaigns that companies increasingly mount in building their corporate brand.

During the dot com boom, of course, the concept of high-octane corporate branding really found its feet in the millions of dollars of ego boosting ads which sought to batter us into submission. I think that, for a brief time, the term for this art was speed branding, or some equally idiotic concoction.

By way of mitigation, it was not wholly unreasonable for some of these supposed egotists to behave this way. Brands such as Yahoo!, or services like my own beenz.com – didn't actually have anything to sell to consumers. We needed their attention, though, to broker it on to our corporate customers. Others, however, did not have this excuse.

Pets.com was typical of the crop in 2000, the height of the boom in speed branding. Armed with IPO proceeds and a fine looking corporate marketing director poached from Procter and Gamble, it spent, for example, $2 m to buy a spot in the Superbowl that year – not including the cost of making the ad or paying the agency (TBWA/Chiat/Day). The highlight was a talking sock puppet – a favourite technique of this agency who also gave the world the Taco Bell Chihuahua. Both won ad industry accolades, but – for pets.com at least – not much business. Since the sock puppet was taken off the leash late in 1999, the company spent more than $3.50

on marketing and sales for every dollar it generated in revenue. A total of $76.6 m was spent on promotion between October through June 2000, against $21.6 m in revenue. Each new customer was costing $240 to acquire. By November 2000, pets.com had gone bust.

So, yes, the dot coms turned corporate branding into a contact sport with insolvency practitioners. But that doesn't mean that other, more reputable and responsible corporations haven't also caught the bug. Or that they can necessarily keep their spending in check.

One corporation, amongst many, which recently indulged itself in this way in the UK was Honda. The manufacturer usually restricts itself to promoting its cars, and has had a record no better or worse than any of its competitors in doing so. At one point, it tried to persuade consumers that the Civic, its bread-and-butter car assembled in the UK – was as British as they were. In the second quarter of 2002, however, Honda tried a new tack; it conspired with its agency to use high profile TV advertising to create a new image for itself as a company. There were no cars near the camera or the script. Just some flabby meanderings about how great it would be if people didn't put up with things being just OK. One assumes that Honda will be helping to banish mediocrity, then. They already started, too. In February 2002, they launched the Jazz, a small people carrier. It has magic rear seats, according to the company, and a digital readout for fuel consumption. OK!

Somewhere between pets.com and Honda, one would hope (being business virtuous) to find real evidence of the financial benefits to corporations of investing such large sums in their corporate image, over and above activities designed directly to stimulate sales. It's a faint hope. I haven't been able to find any data, but then perhaps there's a reason why: there isn't any. If you are looking for business virtue in corporate branding, you won't find it.

Take the fact that corporate branding activity is measured, if at all, in awareness or attitudes, not sales. When Verizon, the US telco, launched its big corporate branding effort in April 2002 (theme: progress; visual: amputee climbing a rope), one industry analyst explained the logic thus. The campaign, he said, 'is about helping people feel good about themselves and what they do, and that Verizon is there to help them do that'.

It's hard to know how to measure something as vague as the association people have between feeling good about themselves and their choice of telephone company. It's impossible to quantify quite what business benefit this might have. So much so, in fact, that one has to wonder quite why corporations such as Verizon – who face tough trading conditions – should indulge a vice as expensive as this. The answer, should you care to quiz them, is usually the same: investment in the brand. The brand, please note, but not the business. Big difference.

SALES PEOPLE ARE FROM MARS, MARKETERS ARE FROM VENUS

There's one big flaw in this plan for restoring business virtue to advertising: the way we divide sales and marketing functions into departments with separate budgets and, more often than not, independent lives. Dividing the labour of revenue generation in this way is an axiom of modern corporate design – accepted without question, implemented without hesitation and maintained with the utmost diligence. It's an arrangement that all but ensures that corporate convenience will take precedence over business logic when tough strategic decisions need to be taken.

However you try to dress it up, sales and marketing people neither understand nor respect what each other does. The one is from Mars: results driven, personally accountable for meeting their revenue goals. The other is from Venus, unable to quantify results most of the time and never held to specific returns because of this – and also because of the high failure rate of their work. Sales people find virtue in deals struck, marketing people in awards won. Sales people make money. Marketing people spend it. Not a good basis for a healthy relationship in many – perhaps most – corporations.

Looked at this way, it's no wonder so many companies strive to keep the two functions well apart – even if this harms the revenue generation which should, after all, be their joint task.

Why this is so becomes obvious looking at, say, those drug companies. Bristol-Meyers' sales of Pravachol suffered by neglecting the traditional, face-to-face, sales channel. The company tried to choose between sales and marketing, and lost. On the other hand, when Schering-Plough launched an equally expansive direct-to-consumer advertising campaign for Claritin, it maintained its direct sales activity to prescribers – and now has the market dominance it sought.

Bottom line: the business logic of making sales and marketing operate together as revenue generators is more compelling, but not always as salient as the corporate logic of keeping them at sword's distance. You can make for company virtue in the purchasing of advertising by avoiding wasteful self-indulgences like corporate branding, and by taking more control over the process yourself. Just don't ever think there's a choice between sales and advertising.

SELF TEST: VICE OR VIRTUE?

Usual rules apply. One point if you agree, none if you don't.

1   Product advertising that builds awareness is just as valuable as a campaign designed to generate sales.
2   Corporations have a straight choice to make between an advertising-led and a sales-led marketing strategy.
3   Advertising should be left to the professionals, which always means hiring in an agency to follow a brief.
4   Some advertising techniques are inherently risky, but they are the best there are and this is reflected in the price and the need to spend more on them, for longer, to achieve the desired result.
5   Corporate brand values can and should be communicated independently of a company's products so that people can have a relationship with them of greater depth than just buying stuff from them.
6   Revenue generation can be either sales- or advertising-led, but not jointly. These disciplines are as different as finance and legal, so effective strategies ensure that we prioritize between them correctly – or let them operate independently to their own strategic goals.

How did you score?

- If you agreed with more than half of the statements, either this chapter went right over your head (for which I apologize) or you must have a big ad budget to play with and lots of agencies pitching for your business. Enjoy.
- If you agreed with about half of the statements, well done; you're on the way to understanding the business virtue of advertising to sell and making sure you get a return.
- If you agreed with less than half of the statements, either I am very persuasive, or you just got laid off from a job in advertising, for which, my condolences.

CHAPTER 6

Shortcuts

I T WAS BOUND TO END IN TEARS. In April 2002, Bernie Ebbers and his hand-tooled cowboy boots tiptoed out of WorldCom, the long-distance telecommunications company he had founded twenty years earlier in a Mississippi diner. Bernie was in a hurry to get big, and bought his way to making WorldCom worth over $170bn at the beginning of 1999. In all, he acquired more than 75 other corporations on the way. Bernie made a lot of people rich, and they loved him for it.

The king of the shortcut, Ebbers didn't do business: he did deals. WorldCom's press people wanted you to know that this guy loved deal-making as much as life itself. Their honed legend even had him singing about Kansas as he entered the head offices of Sprint on his way to try to buy them (he failed).

On the day Bernie left its employ, WorldCom was sweating under a $30bn debt and falling profits as the deal-making caught up with it. The shares were now worth 4% of their 1999 value. A small margin for error might see them disappear altogether. And they were not the only ones. Vodafone, another acquisitive telco whose growth was fuelled by deals rather than by customers, fell below £1 a share in London and slid ever closer to delisting.

Big deals are sexy. Always have been, always will be. The more trailing zeros, the more column inches will be generated. But this doesn't make them good business. Nor are a few other shortcuts most beloved of impatient corporations and their investors. What are they, and why do they persist?

SHORTCUT 1: BUY YOUR COMPETITORS

Don't have the time to wait for your competitors to pack up and go home as you demolish them with your superior product or service? Fear not. Just raise lots of money and buy them out. Yes, you can take years off your business plan in one bold move – and score a bonus from grateful investors. Finance available on favourable terms. Gentle souls need not apply.

This first shortcut is that of acquiring other companies' businesses rather than building your own. This is the route to glory taken by World-Com and so many others with access to too much of other people's money. In the second quarter of 2000, the global trade in companies reached an all time high of $1.3 trn dollars. Down in the dumps in early 2002, however, it was back to 1996 levels at less than a quarter of a trillion dollars' worth of deals being done to March.

So, the acquisition market is cyclical, not terminal. The appetite for buying other companies as a shortcut to growth will almost certainly return with vigour once trading picks up again. And why not? Well, for one thing, if you really want to grow your business, acquiring someone else's isn't often the smart way to do it.

In a startling admission in 2002, McKinsey's very active mergers and acquisition practice admitted that 'numerous studies have shown that M&A destroys value for the acquiring company at least half of the time', and that (shock, horror): 'some observers characterize the motives behind many of these transactions, particularly the largest and most notorious, as mere financial engineering or ego boosting'.

It's not hard to see why said unnamed observers would want to question the personal motives of the deal-makers themselves. The praise routinely heaped upon corporate leaders who take to buying their way to greatness falls only slightly short of hagiography, if at all. They are called visionaries in an age quite unused to miracles. They receive the benefits of political patronage such as a seat in the House of Lords or a place in a Presidential cabinet. Everyone wants them on their board. They get invited to the best parties and can be seen any night of the week with beautiful young women who should know better. And then there's the money. Sir Chris Gent probably didn't go for the parties, but he did get the knight-hood and his multi-million-dollar bonus was for acquiring businesses, not running them profitably.

Nice work if you can get it, of course. Suspected Napoleon complexes aside, the overactive CEOs are not enough to explain why so many com-panies take this perilous path of acquiring their way to an early grave. For one thing, their shareholders don't stop them. Many, such as Chris Gent, act under direct instruction from their boards, their plans nodded along or even goaded by financial analysts who need little persuading that the acquisition shortcut looks like a good one to take.

For some reason, everyone wants to believe that you can create big value from big acquisitions, and would of course love to discover the formula for success. Never one to take things lying down, those busy chaps at McKinsey studied 5000 deals (mostly in the big-dealing, high-tech sector), took dozens of interviews, and explored a bunch of case studies to confirm that whilst 'the *average* merger or acquisition destroys value for the acquirer', some didn't.

Those deals which do work out for the business involved are not the big corporate inflators so beloved of those with an acquisitive temper, such as Bernie Ebbers. Boring is, in fact, better. Making a regular number of small acquisitions to acquire something of value to you appears to work. Cisco Systems, for example, is well known for acquiring small, often start-up, companies which have developed technologies of use to it. This way, they don't take the risk on long-term research and development, or taking on someone else's customers and employees. Nor do they mortgage their entire business and tie up their executives in financial adventurism which is as likely to fail as to succeed. It's so run of the mill in Seattle and Silicon Valley now that consciously shaping your company to make it an easy morsel for Cisco or, say, Microsoft is a point of honour in many hi-tech business plans.

The sad truth is that these dreary dealings are marginalia for the high-rolling world of corporate finance. And whilst most acquisitions have no such obvious business logic, and much higher risk, still no one stops them. To understand why not, look at the deal making from the point of view of the shareholders whose money is apparently being shredded. It all looks very different.

The answer to the question of why investors don't stop the deal-makers making such a mess of things may be that the investors often don't care. It's not that we're all dead in the long run, but that we've cashed in and gone elsewhere.

It doesn't usually take long for shareholders to see a return on a planned acquisition, which is rather the point. Another piece of research by McKinsey found that five days after the announcement of an acquisition plan, your stock price is likely to be up around 2.65% from before the announcement. That's not a bad profit for just putting out a press release. By the way, it appears that only acquisitions make markets smile so. Mergers hardly raise an eyebrow, and joint ventures usually take stock prices down by over 3%. So if you want to bump up a stock, announce that it's going shopping.

A figure of 2.65% doesn't sound exciting enough to explain a trillion dollar vice for the acquisition shortcut, but roll out the acquisition announcements often enough and you can pile these little boosts up and make them last. McKinsey found, for example, that from 1996 to 2001, Heineken bought enough companies in the European beer market to accumulate those post-announcement bumps in their stock price to add a total of 12% to the company's value. Not bad for just talking about what you're going to do, without actually having done it – or made it work. Don't forget that Bernie Ebbers bought over 70 companies and, without the revenues to support it, increased the value of his company shares to dot com levels.

The message is that bad deals make share prices go up not because they're bad but because they're deals. There's more to this than irrational exuberance – the oft-used sick note for capital markets which appear to be off colour. Healthy capital markets are supposed to allocate money efficiently by pricing companies according to their economic performance, not their ability to buy each other.

If valuation were based upon performance, then if a company is growing because business is good, for example, it should be a better investment than one which isn't, therefore attracting buyers for its stock and pushing up the price. When markets do the opposite and attach greater value to companies like Amazon which lose money than to profitable companies like GE, people should be allowed to scratch their heads and wonder if the market is, somehow, broken. In the search for someone to blame, many fingers were pointed at the stock analysts whose recommendations fuelled the market's desire for more, bigger, deals. Indeed, even as WorldCom stock was standing at its perilous high, the bank selling $5 bn of its bonds to help fund Bernie's shopping trips was describing the shares as 'dirt cheap'. Six months later, they were too. Be careful what you wish for.

It's not true, of course, that the market is broken or that it is systematically rigged by mendacious analysts. Market forces are just too strong, too intransigent, to be so controlled. By and large, capital markets have shown that they are moved by more important things than acquisition announcements. They do rise and fall broadly in line with real corporate economic health, in productivity and earnings, but you have to stand back quite a way to see this.

Over a twenty year period, from early 1980 to the end of 1999, including quite a bit of business cycle ups and downs and at least one bubble, the

S&P Index – one of the leading American stock market thermometers – rose by 14% year on year. In the next 18 months it lost nearly 20% of its value. Irrational exuberance, perhaps, but not entirely perverse either. When the market was growing, so were profits: by 2000, earnings per share were $56, up from $15 in 1980. When they fell, so did stocks. Together with fair weather in the economy, over half of the S&P increase is accounted for by inflation-adjusted growth in company revenues. When earnings fell, so did the market.

But our vice for taking the acquisition shortcut means that a larger part of market activity than ever before is now led by corporate deals, not related to business growth. It's worth noting that corporate debt – mostly to fund these deals – was at historically high levels before the current downturn began. At the same time, the deal-making has pushed corporate valuations into a new orbit. In 1999, shares in the 30 companies in the S&P with the highest market value traded at nearly 50 times their company earnings. In 1980, they traded at just 9 times earnings.

These companies could never justify their valuation in returns through higher earnings. Hence the need to pull off the big deals, and the pressure from investors to do so. Some might think that it's greed, wanting to make a fast buck. It is, a bit. But it's also realism. If the market went backwards, and companies began trading closer to their 1980 ratios, most investors would have lost their money anyway. No wonder they don't seem to have any objection to just giving it a go. It's worth thinking about next time a corporate finance specialist wonders aloud if the company oughtn't be seeking to make acquisitions in order to meet this year's growth target.

SHORTCUT 2: PAY YOUR CUSTOMERS TO DO BUSINESS WITH YOU

Entering a new market? Worried that others might come in after you and beat you up? Are you concerned that your market share isn't growing fast enough and that you may not meet your earnings targets this year? Never mind – there is a shortcut. Simply pay your customers to do business with you. You get the revenues, and you keep your share price high enough to see through this challenging period. Everyone wins!

Or not. Paying your customers to do business with you is a shortcut you have to try very hard with if you want to be able to pass if off as good business sense. But try we do.

Take the idea of first mover advantage which most people appear to think entitles them to take any risk, and pay any price, to secure a magnificent share in any new market. For first mover advantage says that to win in a new market, you need to be not just the first in, but the fastest. Get big or die it says, and with a threat like that hanging over them it is no wonder that corporations will happily suspend sound commercial judgement as they race out the door to stake their claim.

It works for some people. Those companies held up as triumphs of the first mover principle, such as eBay (an online auctioneer) and Cisco are genuinely successful companies. And the benefits which can accrue to the first mover are not limited to bleeding edge technology companies and ne'er-do-well dot coms. Coca-Cola practically invented its industry. Häagen-Dazs was a marketing experiment in selling mass-luxury ice cream which created a global industry niche. In each case, the company which was first in has proven to be the longest lasting. If it doesn't own the market any more, it is certainly one its leading brands and dominant forces. Furthermore, first movers are often able to repeat the trick. After it was introduced in 1982 to a sceptical public, and market, within two years Diet Coke had become the third best selling drink in America. Only the sugar-rich titans Pepsi and original Coke itself sold more. Proof positive, then, of the value of being a first mover? Not entirely.

Before you buy into the success stories and use them in your business plan, beware. You are probably about to bet a large piece of your corporate assets, and reputation, on the longest odds in town. Even to play at all, the bet required is sometimes large enough to make the difference between survival and failure.

The fact is, first mover disadvantages almost always outweigh the benefits, even (or especially) in the long term. That is because the shortcuts a company must use to reach and sustain a dominant position faster than normal trading would allow are highly likely never to be recouped. That's why, even after they reach the top, many first movers find they still can't make any money.

BSkyB, Rupert Murdoch's subscription digital TV service in the UK, is a good case in point. When Sky entered the digital satellite market around 1998 it had two things between it and an established first mover advantage. One was the need to migrate its analogue customers to digital, and the other was the more urgent problem of competition with the rival, ONdigital. Both launched in the same month into a virgin market with propositions so similar it was very unlikely that customers could tell the difference between the two.

Stuart Prebble, who resigned as chief executive of ITV Digital (as ONdigital became) in May 2002 when it went bust, wrote soon after that, 'the revolutionary technology was in a race to market'. It soon became clear that Sky was considering giving away the set-top boxes and satellite dishes needed to receive its signal – usually priced at several hundred dollars. And when Sky began to buy its customers, so did ONdigital – doubling the peak capital requirement of launching the company.

In the end, of course, Sky saw off ONdigital with style. After a half-hearted rebranding and a spat over soccer broadcasting rights that it had let itself pay over the odds for, the terrestrial competitor called in the liquidators. Sky had sought, and achieved, first mover advantage. Yet it still loses money on almost every customer, thanks in large part to the opening bribe of a free digibox. Worse still, consumers have rejected the tempting offer of shopping through interactive services which, it was hoped, would bring in those much needed revenues. They have lately developed a $46 m habit for betting on the horses with their remote controls, but this is unlikely to be enough. Sky has paid for over five million customers on whom it is hard to make a profit.

BSkyB and other loss-making first movers, such as Amazon.com, offer the free market equivalent of good old deficit spending by governments who want to fight off a recession with a dose of artificial sweeteners.

Amazon.com, poster child of the internet retailing sector, bought its overwhelming US market share by cutting margins on the books it sold so thin that any profit made on a sale stopped being a mark-up and became an accounting error. Jeff Bezos, Amazon's CEO, even boasted about this to impress investors with his adherence to the first mover religion. He has been so dedicated to capturing market share that outside the US, Amazon got big quick by acquiring other retailers and then cutting prices – a double whammy to its bottom line.

Amazon.com has sales of $3 bn a year and still contrives to make a loss doing it. Worse still, as revenues increase, so do net losses – to over $1 bn in 2002. It promises operating profits by the end of 2003, but bookmakers' odds are not shortening on it going bust beforehand. Even if Amazon survives, it may take decades before investors see an actual return on their capital, so deep is the pool of red ink in which this company now swims. Such is the price, and the dubious value, of taking shortcuts to secure first mover advantage.

It's hard to find anyone for whom the first mover shortcut of paying customers to do business with them has really worked, but this alone won't stop people from trying so long as paying the customer to do business with you guarantees a round of applause from the gallery. If something like this is on your mind, there is an antidote. Just ask yourself what'll happen not if you fail, but if you succeed.

SHORTCUT 3: FORM AN ALLIANCE

I'd never heard of a Barney deal until I entered into one. Somewhere behind a strip mall south of San Francisco, I met the very bright, very excitable executive team of a marketing technology dot com. I was selling an incentive currency; they were selling a service needing an incentive. We had similar customers, and equally punishing revenue expectations. So we talked about and shared our plans, drew on whiteboards and tore through flipcharts. We even got other execs on the conference phone to seek their input. We did all those wholesome things two businesses do when they meet for the first time over a conference table and shook hands on a plan to do things together.

On the way out, my counterpart shook my hand and said, 'I like this. This isn't going to be a Barney deal'. I asked what that was. Barney is a kids' character, a funny purple dinosaur who jumps on stage, waves, and then everyone says how much they love each other. He dances around, but nothing ever really happens. At that moment I knew, of course, that a Barney deal was exactly what this one would be. It was, too. Not that this mattered. We got some nice press notices for it, which wasn't a bad return on one afternoon's work.

After the shortcuts of buying your competitors or your customers, forming an alliance seems tame by comparison. That doesn't mean it's a trivial alternative, though. Accenture thinks that by 2004, 40% of the total market value of 25% of all companies will be for activities they do in partnership with someone else – worth as much as $40 trn.

So when large corporations with enough cash to buy a small country choose an alliance over an acquisition or merger, people pay attention. Car companies, for example, have an apparently endless appetite for each other and billions of dollars change hands as they indulge. So when Renault took a one-third stake in Nissan, rather than just acquiring or merging, and called it an alliance, many were dismayed. They were, frankly, shocked when Renault made the alliance work. Indeed, the fact that they did so was remarkable enough to spawn academic studies and more than one book, not to mention a Harvard Business School case study.

According to a late 1990s study of corporate alliances by Booz·Allen & Hamilton, corporate alliances in the US had grown by 25% a year for the whole of that decade. They reported even higher growth in Europe and Asia. Other studies showed that e-alliances, between high tech firms, were even more rampant.

Not all of them are Barney deals, designed to fail, or at least to go nowhere. It's hard to tell from the outside, though, and almost impossible to do so at the time. This may be part of the reason that stock markets don't like them. The same McKinsey study which worked out the bonus from announcing an acquisition also discovered that five days after an alliance announcement is made, most companies are 3% or more lighter in their valuation.

The main reason markets don't like alliances much is more prosaic. The fact is, they don't work. Popular though they might be, alliances are easy to announce and extremely difficult to do well out of. Alliance-based business might get to be worth $40 trn or so in a few years, but Accenture also counted the collateral damage: as many as 90% of alliances never get off the ground, and of those which do see the light of day, only 2% survive for more than four years.

One reason alliances don't work is the difficulty of pinning down the apparent benefits without, at the same time, undermining the case for an alliance rather than something a little more solid. Not being a merger, cost savings are unlikely, as neither partner is about to give up their head office, employees or cash reserves to their new found friend. If anything, alliances are more likely to increase costs in the short term as deals done by executives have to face the reality of a hierarchy of strangers. Productivity is not likely to be enhanced by hiving off whole teams of people to form a steering group, or by allocating hundreds of hours and more than a few plane rides helping the management teams get to know each other better.

Markets have other reasons to distrust the claims made for alliances. Some of them are just too good to be true. Even though the parties don't expect theirs to be a Barney deal, sometimes they do just turn out that way.

Take, for example, the ill-fated alliance between British Telecom (BT) and AT&T, known as Concert. The idea was to provide high-end data and other communications services to multinationals – on paper, a not unrealistic prospect. Global customers, it was reasoned, would prefer to deal with a global supplier rather than stitch together a patchwork of local offerings. When it was announced in 1998, with fireworks, Concert could claim to have a presence wherever the partners did – and it could do so without anyone having to open a single new office.

Within a year, things were beginning to unravel. There had been management changes and reports of conflict within Concert itself and revenues were said to have disappointed both parties. Each soon had other, more pressing problems to occupy their minds. For its part, AT&T had placed a $110 bn bet on broadband, buying and upgrading as many cable infrastructures as it could. Two profits warnings had already been issued as hoped-for revenues from the new business looked less likely to materialize. BT was in better shape, but not much. Caught between regulator enforced price cuts and cherry picking competition at home, it had spent money with abandon on ambitious plans to become a global force, ending up with the booby prize of a $40 bn debt.

Concert was, in the end, more trouble that it was worth and everyone went their separate ways – much to the relief, no doubt, of many involved. Therein lies the impossibility of using alliances as a shortcut. If an alliance is worth making, because each party sees a compelling reason to do it, the question is why be so tentative? Since alliances are, by definition, less binding than a merger or acquisition – or even a joint venture – why would a company opt to leave itself so vulnerable to losing a valuable chunk of business should the other side walk away. On the other hand, if the idea of forming an alliance – rather than anything more formal – is precisely to allow one or other to suck it and see, then neither side has the courage of its convictions and, like BT and AT&T, are unlikely to take the pain which may be necessary to see it through.

Bottom line: don't think too long about the offer of an alliance which looks like a good shortcut to a better market position, or even a new one. If the business is worth having, it's worth working for, waiting for, or maybe even paying for. Unless, of course, all you have in mind is a turn for Barney on stage.

SELF TEST: VICE OR VIRTUE?

One point if you agree, nothing if you don't.
Do you agree or disagree with the following statements:

1   Acquiring competitors is a smart way to build market share quickly, something which is often reflected in the price.

2   There's no point buying very small companies as their low value won't do anything to increase our market position.

3   Markets move too fast these days to wait on organic growth. Unless you get big enough, fast enough, no corporation will have the strength to survive.

4   Revenues come first: profits can wait. It is worth investing money in building your revenue base, in order to see real returns in future years when the business is locked in.

5   In new and risky markets, alliances work because they offer a fast, low risk, low cost alternative to mergers and acquisitions.

6   Forming alliances impresses investors who can see that you are taking new ideas seriously and exploiting opportunities without blowing their money on ill-advised acquisitions and tricky mergers.

How did you score?

- If you agreed with all of the statements, you must have spent more time than me around conference tables in Silicon Valley. I recommend you drink fewer cans of Tab and try reading this chapter again.
- If you agreed with more than half of the statements, you understand that even if a shortcut gets you there quicker, it may still not be worth taking.
- If you agreed with less than half of the statements, you're obviously a cautious type who should avoid working in investment banking. Sometimes, the shortcut is the point, even though it may not look like such a good idea at the time.
- If you agreed with none of the statements, then you must go to Silicon Valley. There's a reason why that little stretch of desert is the world's most productive economy.

CHAPTER 7

Mis-calculated Risks

P HILIP WATTS, THE CHAIRMAN OF ROYAL DUTCH/SHELL, has a few ideas about what the world might look like in 2020, which he is very eager to share with us. For the past three decades, Shell has produced a pamphlet of scenarios for the future offering 'challenging, coherent, and credible alternative stories about the future'. *People and Connections*, this year's offering, is heady stuff, and an important contribution, so says Philip, to helping businesses plan for the future.

You can imagine, therefore, the excitement which attends the arrival of this document in your in-tray every three years. Open it and you see the big trends, long trends in birth rates, consumption of fossil fuels, the spread of literacy, the use of this technology and the decline of that. Scientific, detailed and obviously trustworthy, it's Faith Popcorn with a calculator.

It's so thrilling, the thought of getting your teeth into the scenarios themselves ('not predictions', emphasizes the introduction – like we're going to believe them). This year those whizzes at Shell have settled upon just two possible futures for us to choose from, but they are utterly different. I am hoping, as I read it, to be able to divine which second language my children ought to learn. Right now, it's between Chinese and Spanish. So which will it be?

In the first scenario, 'Business Class', the world is run by an 'interconnected global elite', operating a highly globalized (read: homogeneous) economy in a 'New Medievalism' in which the nation state is almost redundant as multinational trade and corporations set their own rules. I should have my kids learn Spanish, then, and for career purposes ensure that they get into INSEAD, where the global elite gets its MBA.

In the second scenario, 'Prism', people reject internationalized, homogenized, cultures and renew their respect for local institutions and identities. Instead of globalization, where economic efficiency means us all doing the same thing in the same way, we get 'multiple modernities' which might be less efficient but make us all happier. Second language choice would probably be Chinese, in this case, and business school can be skipped in favour of backpacking on a Boeing sonic jumbo.

Sadly, if you are looking for a tip from Philip Watts as to which of these worlds we will be living in, you will be disappointed. In an unspeakably cruel ending, the audience is not allowed to find out who did it, or even whether Shell itself is planning for a Business Class or a Prism world. They don't even know if, twenty years from now, they will be selling us fuels which still have to be dug out of the ground. What use it that?

Feeling let down by this obvious lack of faith in their own predictions, I wonder whether this entire exercise is just a fabulous corporate prank by Shell at our expense. And if it is, someone should tell those other companies which have adopted the Shell system to stop now, before they make greater fools of themselves. This is unlikely, however: no joke can run for this long – thirty odd years – without being found out.

Every business investment decision involves some kind of bet upon the unknown future – at odds that will always seem better when the future is described by someone, or with some method, we find we can believe in.

So it is more likely that Shell's futurology and the gravitas with which others receive and imitate it is the offspring of a collective corporate vanity, an unshakeable belief in one's own cleverness and power to see ahead in order to avoid groping forward in the pitch black and bumping into things.

Upon this vanity rests a corporate vice for predictions of any kind. The business danger of accepting such prophecies is clear. One can find a prediction to suit any risk you wish to take, from equally credible sources with similar supports and certainties. Predictions don't reduce risk, they merely make us more comfortable with them.

PROPHECIES OR FUTURES?

Corporate futurology goes in cycles. At times the fashion is for prophets and oracles – some person or thing possessed of a certainty about the future and willing to let you in on the secret. The 1990s investment bubble was a good time for oracles – everyone from stock analysts to economics professors were blessed with 20/20 foresight that was in demand everywhere from Wall Street to Downing Street. When events proved these prophets false, their further predictions lost currency. Quickly, we rediscovered scientific, or worldly, methods of prediction. We wanted equations rather than visions – futures rather than prophecies.

Right now we are very much in the scientific part of the futurology cycle. Hence, for example, Shell's emphasis on their numbers and their scenario building methodology. Not for them the anointing of seers; although the chairman provides the introduction, he does not claim the scenarios for himself. Objectivity is everything. The scenario building process claims to be a clinical extrapolation of facts and figures which are by themselves uncontroversial. You can go in and check their sums if you're not sure.

So oracles are out of fashion, and some are even on their way to court where the people who lost money on their prophecies are after a bit of payback. For the next few years, the calculator will be king. But this doesn't mean more accurate predictions; far from it.

THE PROBLEM WITH SAMPLING

Hitherto, all methods of predicting the future scientifically have rested upon a conception of probability almost unchanged since the 17th Century. Until recently, in fact, simple probability has been the only alternative to taking a visit to your local psychic, who is unlikely to tell you that you have a 93.2% chance of meeting your future spouse in the next thirty days, or your money back.

Peter Bernstein has probably thought more about this area of business life than anyone alive. He wrote the book on it: *Against the Gods*, which provides a complete social and commercial history of basing decisions on calculations of the likelihood of things happening or not.

Using maths to predict the future is, Bernstein shows, all about the quality of information available to you when you place your bet. For quality, read sampling. Since perfect knowledge is only obtainable after the fact, beforehand one has to make do with a small piece of it from which to make predictions. The trick is to know when the sample you have is good enough to support an accurate prediction.

Knowing for certain when your sample is good, however, is impossible. The only sample which is 100% accurate is the whole universe. So anything less is a matter of opinion, or of budget. If you can only afford to sample five hundred people in your market research, all you can do is cross your fingers and hope it's good enough. You'll find out, eventually. When it's too late, that is. Doubtless the marketers at Coca-Cola must have thought that the 200,000 people who tasted their new formula Coke was a big enough sample. Clearly, it wasn't.

Market research never quite recovered from that debacle. Although companies such as MORI and Gallup would point to their revenues to claim otherwise, the fact is that the Coke affair, and more than a few miscalls on elections, have taken the shine off simple probability as an infallible tool for guiding your business decisions, especially where people are involved.

One company which found this out at great expense and considerable embarrassment was the British supermarket, Safeway. The whole grocery sector has got religion when it comes to statistics. Tesco, which is currently the UK's number one chain, even went so far as to buy Dunnhumby (slogan: 'essential customer genius'), the company it had hired to do its predictions for it, just to stop anyone else having a bite at the cherry.

Safeway had data which predicted that 20% of consumers would switch supermarket if given a chance to save a mere 1% on their shopping. 15% of shoppers change their main supermarket every year anyway; all they needed was a push to come in Safeway's direction. That was offered in the form of the ABC discount card which offered consumers the required 1% cash discount which they accumulated on their cards and could take advantage of whilst shopping.

The prediction was wrong. Even though a sizeable, representative sample of shoppers in the key demographic said they'd switch to Safeway, they did anything but. Not one to be put off by this experience, Safeway carried out further research a few years later when they wanted to ditch the scheme. 73% of cardholders admitted that losing it wouldn't affect their shopping habits. That turned out not to be true either. Just one year after the timely demise of Safeway's ABC program, profits across the company were up 31% on increased sales of nearly 10%.

THE LATEST FROM IOWA

This time round, traditional statistical methods face a new threat, other than their own incompetence. When it comes to finding clever reasons for doing stupid things, they've got Iowa to contend with.

Iowa is the unlikely epicentre of the latest fad in prediction techniques – the artificial market. The Iowa Electronic Market is operated by the business school at the university there as a teaching aid, but it has also spawned a small industry of predictive services using their ideas. Since it started in 1988, the IEM has predicted not only election outcomes, but the size of majorities, to degrees of accuracy which professional polling organizations find hard to match.

Participants pay real money to buy contracts on possible events, such as election results, but also now on movie takings, corporate earnings reports and monetary policy decisions by the Federal Reserve. The price of contracts are bid up or down with demand. So, as the 2000 presidential election drew to a close, the price of Gore shares converged with Bush shares – the eventual victor being four cents a share more expensive in the last days before voting.

Why should this work? One reason is, of course, that it is close enough to real-life markets to be touched by the hidden hand itself. Markets are able to set prices by aggregating the individual preferences of all participants. If more people want to sell than buy, the price will fall until enough buyers enter the market, or enough sellers pull out, to exactly match demand to supply.

You can see these processes at work in real time as a trader on the IEM. Say more people fancied Mike Bloomberg to win the New York mayoral election than his opponent, the price of his futures would have gone up. The degree to which the price moved would reflect the aggregated strength of feeling. If people weren't sure, as in the presidential run-off, the prices of stocks in the candidates would not be expected to diverge by much. This is exactly what happened.

True to the times, and to its almost mythical reputation as a revolutionary discovery for corporate futurology, the IEM has many imitators. You can play the odds (for free, thankfully) on who will win Oscars on the Hollywood stock exchange, which claims 400,000 accounts. You can go to Foresight Exchange and buy a future on anything from a cure for AIDS by 2005 or the real-life arrival of ET by 2050. Commercial services can now offer your company a chance to predict the success or failure of your strategy or product, by placing it on any one of several global markets hosted on the Internet. Or, of course, you could just throw out your Shell scenarios and pick the highest priced future.

It was a fair prediction that Bob Worcestor, the founder of MORI, would hate all this stuff. 'We must get half a dozen offers to go into business with these each week, and we always show them the door', he told *New Scientist* magazine. His particular beef with artificial markets is what he considers to be a lack of statistical integrity. There is no guarantee, for example, that the high price of contracts attached to Elvis being alive means it's probably true. It may just mean that a lot of Elvis fans have found this market. 'They're voodoo polls', he says.

It's a bit rich for a statistician like Bob Worcestor to pick on artificial markets because of the unreliability of their samples, when his industry has shown itself to be just as vulnerable to asking the wrong thing to the wrong people. If you have ever commissioned any market research, you'll know that what you get back has three numbers: the raw number of people asked, the margin for error, and the weighted result. This latter is just another way of saying, here's what we think it would be if we'd asked everyone, based upon our other assumptions about the statistical validity of the people we did actually ask. Educated guesswork is guesswork nonetheless.

PLAYING GAMES WITH THE FUTURE

One popular stock on the Hollywood stock exchange in 2002 was for Russell Crowe to win the best actor Oscar for his portrayal of the mathematician John Nash in *A Beautiful Mind*. Nash is a major figure in the development of games theory – like artificial markets, an alternative to probability as a means of predicting the future. It is also more established in the corporate world, and as such considerably more dangerous to your business virtue.

Games theory is more fashionable in some quarters than sex right now, but not as fun. It involves predicting what might happen in a given number of competitive situations, and then working out algebraically which is most likely to actually happen. Once you've figured out what might happen, and ranked the possibilities, you can choose your own path somewhere between the best and worst case scenario. At least, that's the theory. What Nash and others did was to provide the tools for the job. It's up to you to hang yourself.

The language of games theory has infected everyday management thinking. Any prudent manager wants a 'win-win' solution. A rational decision maker would recommend the company pursue the 'optimal scenario'. Any deal-maker who gets a reputation as a 'player' will keep it until too many of his calls don't 'go his way'. Algebra has never been so popular or so misused.

Promising fast solutions to big problems, games theory has attracted many corporate followers for some time. Even back in 2000, a paper published in a reputable economics journal by Hugh Courtney, a McKinsey consultant, had studied its use in over 100 corporations. The author argued that games theory gives decision makers the ability to 'look forward and reason backward'. Crystal balls at the ready.

How does it work? Take a company deciding whether to build a new factory that will increase production capacity by 50%. Mr Courtney believes that 'the best business strategists must be skilled at predicting future rounds of competitive conduct'. They do so by imagining every possible permutation of how competitors, suppliers and customers might react to this decision. Customers might not buy the extra product, driving prices down. Suppliers may not go to some locations, but will to others. Workers may not relocate, or may not need to if local labour is available. Competitors might start a price war, to drive margins below sustainable levels during the investment phase. Every imaginable possibility must be considered. As Mr Courtney says, 'a good game theorist gets inside the heads of other players to understand their economic incentives and likely behaviour'. Now that sounds like fun.

When all of the what-ifs have been considered, the job of the strategist is then to crunch the numbers and work out which of these represents the most rational, or likely, response by each party. If competitors did engage in a price war, would this leave them in financial difficulties? That's not a rational thing to do: it can be discounted. And so on. By the way, this is how computers play chess. They simply try a bunch of permutations of possible moves and choose the one with the highest likelihood of success. When you adjust the difficulty rating, all you are doing is letting the computer play more scenarios with itself with every move. You don't stand a chance, really.

In theory, at least, games theory should work. And so it should: Von Neumann, who is along with Nash one of the fathers of the theory, reserved his strongest feelings for those 'utterly mistaken' wishy-washy romantics who thought that you could not model human behaviour like this. And minus the maths, games theory comes quite close to being able to describe the way some good business strategists actually behave.

How about some pigs for an example. Mr Joseph Luter heads Smithfield, a US meat processing corporation which has a $6 bn annual turnover.

Mr Luter has been in the business so long, he seems to be able to read the minds of his competitors.

The game Mr Luter plays in his pork business would be modelled as what's called the prisoners dilemma. The players in this model have all been arrested during a heist and held in separate cells. If no one snitches, everyone will get a short sentence. If one person rats on the others, he goes free, everyone else gets life. But then what if everyone rats …? To win, you must get far enough into the heads of your competitors to predict what they'll do. Mr Luter does.

In Mr Luter's case, the total market for pork and beef in the US has hardly changed in more than a decade. Margins have been driven down as far they can be without being a mere statistical error. Profits are about 3% overall. So market share is everything. If everyone cooperates, each gets to keep something. Rock the boat, everyone might go down.

But in 1990, Mr Luter went to Europe and discovered that consumers here ate more pork because we had better pigs. Judging that consumers would react faster than the competition to a quality product, Mr Luter loaded 2000 British sows onto a converted jumbo and flew them home. Their descendents now supply half of his meat. Only one player ratted: Mr Luter.

FAST THINKING FOR BAD IDEAS

So much for the practice. The theory, unfortunately, is not so good.

You won't be surprised to discover that there's a big difference between someone like Mr Luter who has a lifetime of personal experience to draw upon in predicting his competitors' moves, and a bunch of bright MBAs in a big room trying to emulate the same with a load of whiteboards and flipcharts. This small fact is somewhat lost on most companies which use games theory in their strategic speed chase. And that's why it hurts them.

The use of games theory by hurried corporations was, for example, to a great extent responsible for one of the largest corporate gambles in recent history: the $250 bn spent by Europe's telecommunications companies on acquiring government licences to operate third-generation (3G) broadband mobile telephone networks.

Most countries operated an auction process to sell their high frequency radio spectrum licences, but the UK went first. A number of spectra were made available and bidders invited. Generally, the highest bidder in each spectrum would win it, although some were reserved for new entrants in order to encourage competition amongst the winners once the services were running. During each round, bidders submitted their best revised offer or took one of their three permitted breaks from bidding.

The results of the UK auction were posted on the Internet as each round progressed. The world was agog as the numbers climbed to jaw dropping levels – to the quiet dismay of investors whose money was being used to run this particular steeplechase. Between each round, the games theorists were advising the bidders on strategy, updating their models of competitor behaviour with the intelligence gathered from the previous round. It was tense. It was also insane.

Some were clearly following sophisticated strategies which only they were privy to: British Telecommunications began by bidding only for one of the licences, but when WorldCom dropped out of the race for a different licence which was also part of the auction, BT began to bid for that, too. The first licence was becoming very expensive, and losing it may not matter if the second licence came through. BT had pushed the price high enough to threaten the viability of Vodafone who were the only other remaining bidder for the first licence, and may still end up with a satisfactory slice of spectrum for itself. The strategy succeeded, at least in one respect: BT won the licence it started to bid on later, at a price of £4 bn. Vodafone got the other, paying almost £2 bn more.

Dismayed by the prices paid at the end of the auction, many investors in these corporations worried out loud that there was no proven demand for this technology to justify the cost. They might also have been concerned that the technology was not even proven, and no one had quantified the cost of implementation. It gets worse. In September 2001, a UK subsidiary of electronics manufacturer, Siemens, announced that it had filed patents on a 'brick' which allowed the high-frequency signals used by these services to pass through home and office walls. Without it, your 3G mobile may not work indoors. Oops.

DOING WITHOUT

Would it be better to try doing without games theory, artificial markets, and statistical modelling altogether? Actually, no. Whatever their faults, these tools offer a far better chance of success than the nearest alternative, a return to oracular individuals with their random interpretations of the future. Any tool can be misused, and these are no exception.

The most common error made when applying any mathematical technique, whether one is using games theory to plan an investment, or buying media on the basis of market research, is how far ahead you ask it to look. Overconfidence in the predictions we receive from our pollsters and artificial markets is the real enemy of good judgement.

A good proof of the myopia of predictions, for example, can be found in the highly volatile fashion industry. Nowhere is the need to see ahead greater, or the risk of failure more acute. Even if you get the right style blouse in for your summer season, you can still get the wrong shade or fabric and have to shred it all. For traditionally structured fashion retailers such as Marks & Spencer, whose supply chain is long and slow, by the time it's gone wrong it is nearly always too late to fix it. With only one chance to get it right, the only predictive tool is the eye of your buyers.

Zara has shown it needn't be like this. The European fashion retailer manufactures its own items using a low-volume, but highly flexible production system. Zara introduces around 12,000 different items into its stores every year and does not need to plan much further ahead than the few weeks it takes to go from design to manufacture. For the first time, a major fashion company has found that it can measure sales of individual lines, and use this data to order more or switch to something else mid-season. The higher unit cost implicit in this kind of low volume manufacture is more than offset by the significantly lower failure rate of what it produces. Sales have increased by 30% in each of the past five years.

EGGS AND BASKETS

What is most surprising about the Zara experience is that anyone should find it a revelation. For the intrinsic myopia of any mathematically based predictive technique has been known for fifty years, as has the only effective solution for it: hedging.

In 1952, a little known and largely forgotten 25-year-old graduate student from Chicago called Harry Markowitz wrote an article in the *Journal of Finance* entitled 'Portfolio Selection'. It was a densely mathematical treatment of something you can now buy over the counter at the Post Office, namely, a managed risk investment. The past performance of an investment,

Markowitz believed, is no guarantee of future returns. The greater your expectation, in fact, the greater the risk you run if it goes wrong.

By factoring in the risk attached to poor performance, and holding a number of investments of different degrees of risk, you could treat your portfolio as a whole and predict accurately the total return over time. If you want a higher return, you have to accept a higher risk, and vice versa.

The exact same principles operate in any commercial decision where a prediction of any kind is involved. The further away the event is, the greater the risk attaching to it. Hence the myopia of prediction: if, like Zara, you are only interested in things happening right under your nose, you are dealing with much lower risks than Marks & Spencer, or any retailer with a supply chain that takes months to run its course.

One side effect of myopia is, of course, to put things outside your useful field of vision into soft focus. This is why short sighted people often take off their glasses when they look in the mirror. Whenever you see a corporation like Shell peering so far into the distance, something similar is almost certainly happening. Looking again at their scenarios, I think I can see it too. They want you to know that, whatever happens, Royal Dutch/ Shell will always be there to supply your energy needs. There now, don't you feel so much better for knowing that?

SELF TEST: VICE OR VIRTUE?

Do you agree or disagree with the following statements:

1   It is always important to accurately predict the future as far ahead as possible to inform your strategic thinking.
2   We will never listen to the opinions of futurologists in banks or universities again, particularly after they let us down so badly in the 1990s investment bubble.
3   The only predictions worth anything are those made using proven mathematical techniques.
4   It's only the quality of data that lets down market research techniques, not any fundamental problem with this approach.
5   New techniques for predicting the future, such as artificial markets, are intrinsically reliable because they rely on rational expectations just like real markets and are worth experimenting with in my business.

6   Games theory is a valuable tool for strategic thinking, providing a robust analysis and means of accurately weighing options, based upon the most likely outcomes to any decision.

How did you score?

- If you agreed with all the statements, you must have been to see *A Beautiful Mind* one too many times. The Hollywood stock exchange got the Oscar prediction wrong! Go back and start again.
- If you agreed with more than half of the statements, you may have a degree of healthy scepticism about predictive techniques, but not enough perhaps to stop you trying to see too far into the future to risk making bad business decisions.
- If you agreed with half or less than half of the statements, you are perhaps a little too sceptical. This can be risky, since you are likely to find yourself relying too much on personal opinions and rejecting any kind of analysis out of hand.
- If you agreed with none of the statements, you really ought to go and see *A Beautiful Mind*. Pay particular attention during the bar scene when Nash experiences his games theory epiphany and unlocks the secrets of the universe.

CHAPTER 8

Big IT

S IMON ORME HAS WHAT YOU AND I MIGHT CONSIDER a nice problem to have. One of the UK's most sought after IT marketing consultants, he has been having a harder than usual time helping his latest client find customers for their technology. Even reducing the price to lower the risk hasn't got the fish biting. The issue, he tells me as we near the bottom of a fine claret, is that the product is just too good to be true. Isn't that just the kiss of death?

Simon is not a man much given to overstatement, but he really doesn't help himself by referring to his client's product as the philosopher's stone of corporate IT systems. You can see his point, though. This product is a low cost computer system which writes other software to order.

Honest. Anything you want, you can have. No nerds required. Not a single Gantt chart or project plan. No budget overruns. No bugs. You can generate code on demand which is guaranteed to work exactly as billed, and to be available for installation a matter of hours after asking for it. Need a bespoke system to speed up your warehouse? A CRM package? Some supply chain maintenance? Tell Simon's system what you want, go home to bed, and in the morning it will be done. If the software isn't quite right, tweak the brief and run it again – at no extra cost. Programmers of the world, unite: the computers may be about to put you out of work.

It's not just that companies aren't buying it. They don't even want to hear about it. Those gracious enough to provide comments appear to think Simon must be bonkers, even those who have known him for decades and have never complained before. He and I discuss this distressing situation and we conclude, as we reach the bottom of the wine bottle, that the problem is something much simpler. It's just not expensive enough to be credible. Simon should add a few extra zeros at the end of the price tag.

Big IT is a corporate vice of apparently unstoppable force with an addiction to grand projects and a commitment always to spend more whenever offered less. In the demented logic of corporate IT procurement, a product can be new or it can be cost effective, but never both.

This is not a small problem. First, before the current recession, IT spending accounted for as much as one pound in every six spent by British companies – on average, 50% more of their budget than was allocated for technology ten years ago. The business cycle, peer pressure and government heckling both seem likely to push those figures higher again in the future.

This wouldn't matter, if it worked, a fact about which no one is entirely certain. Overall technology effects are easier to determine than specific items, like IT infrastructure, which often don't directly affect the unit cost of production. Big projects such as CRM systems are much harder to evaluate, as we shall see, than a slick, new, production-line process.

The balance of evidence is, however, not on the side of the vendors of these kinds of systems. Studies by, amongst others, the OECD, have found that corporate IT projects very often fail to deliver a return – either in productivity, or revenue. Big IT is more risky to business virtue than almost anyone, especially the technologists in your company, is ever likely to admit.

IT'S WHAT YOU KNOW

The only way to understand the problems we have with big IT, is to first appreciate the grasp that information has on the corporate testicles.

Commercial information is so dangerous that many advanced capitalist societies reserve greater punishments for insider dealing than they do for corporate manslaughter. Special exclusions are routinely grafted to constitutional guarantees of free speech to allow for companies to keep secrets.

We also have a special place in our hearts for those brilliant, crafty or just lucky people who have been the first to the floor with some priceless nugget – even if the stories are so much flannel. One such well known information fantasy is the story of Nathan Rothschild's market shattering coup at the Battle of Waterloo in 1815. Supposedly, by some means – a carrier pigeon, a fast boat back from the battlefield, stories vary – the family who had bankrolled much of the hostilities were the only people in the market who knew of Napoleon's defeat. They were therefore able to make a killing by going long on British government stock. Not much of this is true, and anyway, as the historian Niall Ferguson found out, 'it is almost impossible to say precisely how the Rothschilds performed financially in this period because they had no idea themselves'. So much for the omniscient Rothschilds. Still, it's amazing the kind of thing we'll believe to support our adoration of information.

Other than news, there's still the more run-of-the-mill stuff; the weights and measures that enable companies to make informed decisions about everything from buying stationery to building new factories. A multi-billion dollar research industry hangs off this ever growing need to find facts to ground your guesswork – and you can expect it to increase if our obsession with speed continues to value decision-making speed over accuracy.

In fact, so important is timely and accurate information to companies that since the mid-1970s corporate culture has decided, as with so much else, not to leave anything about it to chance. In practice, this has meant one thing: computers.

TOO IMPORTANT TO LEAVE TO CHANCE

Once upon a time, before computers took over the work of gathering, processing and analysing information, we had to rely on more primitive, less secular, ways of getting to know the things that mattered.

Information gathering was an art, and quite a laborious one at that. It's heroes were people like the retailer Sam Walton, who spent his weekends visiting his stores around America to get a feel for what was going on there.

Now, however, the company he founded operates the world's largest data processing facility outside the US military. Its job is to crunch numbers on every aspect of every part of the Wal-Mart business. When a toothpaste tube is sold in Missouri, it knows. When you bought that T-Shirt in Florida last summer, they stored it. Wal-Mart has travelled the extremes – from one man with a feeling for floorspace who liked stalking his employees, to one computer which has everyone's, and everything's, number. In three decades, computers – or more precisely, fast processors and relational databases – have engendered an industrialization of knowlege gathering which had led us all on a similar path to Sam Walton and his company. Lazy thinking has stiched these assorted technological advances into an information age which is, of course, nothing of the sort.

WHAT INFORMATION AGE IS THAT, THEN?

You hear it a lot, but it isn't true that ours is an information age. At best, it's a data processing age. Getting to the answer faster is more highly prized than what we are able to do with the information once we have it. There are a few reasons to think this.

First, would an information age really be as obsessed as ours is with the processing power of microchips – and in particular, with the density of transistors etched onto silicon? Probably not. But a data processing age would. Not that it means much, anyway. Anyone in the IT industry will tell you that it doesn't really matter how many instructions your microchip can process each second; if there's a limit, try writing faster software. You can make your computers as fast as you like: it doesn't make you any smarter.

Further proof that this is a data processing, rather than an information, age must surely lie in the amount of money, growing ever greater, which companies invest in their IT capabilities. OK, so things slowed down during the recession from 2001, but no one is projecting a permanent downturn in any part of the technology industry. Early in 2002, the cycle had already restarted: shares in chip makers began to rise as their order books recovered. This can only mean one thing, that their customers were building stock again. Don't write off future IT booms quite yet.

According to the OECD, US corporations spent twice as much in real terms on IT and telecommunications (ICT) in 2000 than they did in 1980, and 32% more than in 1990. UK firms today spend three times more of their budgets on ICT than they did 20 years ago, and 50% more than in 1990. It's still going up, despite the economic conditions: growth rates of 13% per annum in IT spending by British companies in the second half of the 1990s is likely to carry on – thanks particularly to increased investment in software and services. The figures have, since 1993, also included software spending as well as hardware and services. Software alone accounts for 3% of total UK company spending today and grows by 2% each year.

What's more, the extra money spent today buys so much more than it used to: price indices of high-tech equipment have, according to economists, fallen by around 3% a year for each of the last 20 years in the UK and around 1% a year worldwide. It's a good era to be in IT. When it's raining, the happy man is the one selling umbrellas.

IS IT WORKING?

We've been sold on the idea of the information age, but we're increasingly finding that data processing isn't quite the same thing. What's more, it may be the opposite. Oops.

The economist Robert Solow, who won the Nobel Prize for his contributions to the economic theories of growth, once remarked, 'you can see the computer age everywhere but in the productivity statistics'. He's right, but people are only just now beginning to understand how, and why.

First, consider the evidence that all this IT investment isn't making its way through to the bottom line. It's late coming, but getting stronger all the time.

Why are we only finding this out now? The reason we've had to wait so long for it is that economists haven't been able to agree (nothing new there) on how to separate economic growth due to the production of information technology – Microsoft, Oracle and Dell profits – and growth due to increased productivity of companies using it.

They are getting there, though. An OECD paper published in 2001 concludes that, across the OECD member countries, most of the economic growth attributable to IT is accounted for by the growth in IT companies, not through higher productivity of customers using their products. In the UK, the OECD found that the latter group contributed just 0.7% to productivity growth from 1995 to 1999 – despite the huge increase in spending which occurred in that time.

In fact, there are even more pessimistic views out there which also bear a listening. One group has observed a net loss in productivity from IT investments. They call it the IT productivity paradox: more tools, less efficiency. They've put numbers on stuff which most of us already know. Ever tried to make sense of a new, heavy duty IT system? Or got to grips with the latest release of your spreadsheet or contact management software? The immediate effect of new IT investments, even if the software actually works, is to slow everyone down whilst they get to grips with the damn thing.

A study by the OECD in 1999 was able to substantiate this by looking at the experience of over 1000 US firms over a previous decade. The 'learning cost' of new technology explains why, throughout the 1980s, US and UK productivity did not increase markedly despite the heavy investment being made in the technology. It also explains why upgrades don't deliver if you make them too soon: people haven't learnt how to use the last version yet.

Indeed, the damage that this does to corporate performance is even beginning to worry some of the people who were telling you to buy the software in the first place. Attention is increasingly being focused on silver-bullet solutions to business problems promised by technologists but which fail to earn their keep.

Take, for example, the results of a 2001 survey of chief information officers by *CIO Magazine* in the US into the effectiveness, or otherwise, of their all-singing and dancing CRM (Customer Relationship Management) systems.

CRM projects have given us huge data warehouses which crunch raw data on customer behaviour, not to mention the barcodes, loyalty cards and tele-surveys used to hoover in that information in the first place. The promise of CRM is that from data shall come knowledge – and statistical support for doing things to improve the bottom line.

One such system, for example, was able to tell its owner that male shoppers tended to buy both beer and tights on their way home from the office. By putting the two products next to each other the company improved sales of both. Who needs local managers with a gift for merchandising when the computer can do the thinking for them? Will the wonders never cease?

Yes, actually. The respondents to the survey for *CIO Magazine* reported that as many as 70% of all CRM projects had failed to deliver any benefit to the business. This isn't small beer: the average project costs over $2 m dollars and takes over a year to implement. It may also indicate why there are such high levels of disappointment: a third of all CRM projects go over budget, according to a June 2002 survey in the same magazine, and one in ten switch vendors during the process. Even those who have to implement them find CRM projects cost more, take too long and often need fixing even before they start.

It is a lunacy which inspires no great wonder that companies such as Oracle who provide the data processing engines for these operations, are now serving the interests of humanity by targeting most of their R&D on incremental improvements in their databases and operating systems. And others are making headway with systems to compensate for the problems with other systems, whilst others provide more layers on top so you can see what's going on.

Don't rush to sell your shares in Siebel, however, or anyone else who supplies the CRM software market. European firms ploughed $423 m (€397 m) into CRM software in 1999. They don't seem to care yet if it works or not: that figure is expected to rise to $3.5 bn by 2004, according to the Gartner Group. And this from the company which projected, in 2000, that by 2005, 80% of sales force automation projects will be failing – not because of bad technology, but because of the people using them. The learning cost, it seems, just grows with your IT budget.

THE DESKTOP DELUSION

Why haven't companies realised that spending more on big IT can have the opposite effect on their productivity to what they're looking for? The learning cost of IT alone means that the more you invest, the more you stand to lose. And why do companies look like they're just going to keep on doing it?

There are probably a couple of reasons worthy of your consideration.

The first is what one might call the prevailing delusion that by making your employees individually more productive, you make your company more productive. In fact, learning costs aside, the opposite may well be the case. Call this the desktop delusion if you like, after the huge amounts of data processing horsepower which now reside on every employee's desktop – not just through faster, bigger computers but the access which most now have to the information bazaar of the Internet.

So one aspect of the desktop delusion is due to what's commonly called information overload. People's brains have not expanded to fit the information available to them to process. But we're resourceful, and have found ways to make it appear as if they have. The software helps. In many cases, the desktop applications – spreadsheets, databases and raw numerical power can now be used to give the appearance of thoughtful analysis when the machine has done everything for you. It is now possible to perform more complex calculations on a mobile phone than on the computers which took the Apollo spacecraft to the moon.

The desktop delusion has other, more worrying effects. One is that blind faith in the computer tends to allow neglect of other, more proven, methods of making people productive. There's statistical evidence for this, too.

Try plotting the increase in the number of personal computers in a country to the overall change in productivity per worker. If more desktops made for more productivity, you should be able to establish a clear relationship based upon a correlation of these figures. As we get more PCs, we should get more productive, and vice versa. Not a chance.

In the period from 1992 to 1999, the OECD recorded a 43% increase in the penetration of personal computers in the US, and correlated an acceleration in productivity of less than 0.5%. In the UK, on the other hand, there was a 20% increase in PC usage. A slowdown in productivity growth was observed! Ireland had a similar uptake of the grey boxes under their desks. What happened? Nearly 1% acceleration in productivity growth.

If it seems hard to make sense of this, that's because you need to stop thinking that putting computers on desks is more important to making people productive than, say, training and efficiently organizing their efforts. Big IT offers a solution which you can address with money and is delivered in boxes. If only it were the right one.

SUSPEND YOUR DISBELIEF, OPEN YOUR WALLET

Other than the prevailing desktop delusion, there is one other reason for corporations' continued addiction to the potentially dangerous drug of big IT. This you could call the vendorization of investment decisions.

Only a third of IT professionals, according to a survey by *CIO* and *Darwin* magazines in February 2002, actually rely on independent research when making investment decisions. Even this isn't as good as it sounds, because some of the analysts may not be as independent as they may appear. Of those who pay out, on average, half a million dollars each year for independent research, 84% reported themselves to have some level of concern that vendors have undue influence as clients of the researchers. I'm sure I've heard that somewhere before.

Simply put, companies tend to evaluate IT projects based upon a comparison of one vendor's claims against another and the few who do go for independent counsel can't be sure that they're getting gospel. Vendorization is a key part of exploiting corporate weakness for technology. You can see it in action when you look at, for example, how a new trend for something called Web services is establishing itself right before our very eyes.

There's a formula to turning a complex new technology – like Web services – which no one understands, into a cash cow which everyone must have. It's been followed with success more times than one cares to count – from Sun's Java language to Oracle's databases and everything in between. Here's how it works.

First, prepare the ground. Vendors in this stage pose as educators, and get others to back them on the intellectual case for the new product.

Vendors sponsor conferences, but everyone sees through them. Consultants, like CAP Gemini or McKinsey, publish books and try to be objective – even though they are promoting the vendors' cause.

In February 2002, for example, McKinsey offered its clients an online primer to Web services. According to the McKinsey puff, whilst 'players like IBM, Microsoft, and Sun Microsystems have convinced some observers that Web services will soon be a reality … potentially powerful innovations are building behind the buzz'.

Second, get the internal influencers on your side – i.e. the geeks. The smarter vendors, like Microsoft, engage the interest of the technology community early on by giving them access to tools which will allow them to get excited about this new stuff too. So Microsoft, for example, allowed developers into its Web services platform (known as .net) before their bosses got so much as a whiff of a brochure. The benefit of this is clear: when the CEO asks the CTO about this Web services thing, the CTO will be able to say, we've known for ages and we're working on it.

At this point, the real marketing can start, and the normal rules of corporate sales will apply. Tick the right boxes, get the right people behind you. No one will resist the idea for fear of being marginalized in the corporation, and everything is a fight over the detail and the relative merits of competing products. The vendorization of the investment decision is complete: the client knows it wants Web services – the question is: whose to buy?

The resistance to vendorization doesn't come from the business, however. It starts (and stops, mostly) in the IT department itself. If you've ever wondered where the appeal of the open source software movement comes from, this is it.

Open source software – free products like the Linux operating system – appeals greatly to the people working in IT departments who otherwise would face a lifetime implementing someone else's technology and then getting the blame when it doesn't work.

THE RISE AND DECLINE OF THE CIO

How then, to break out of the habits which have promised an information age, and delivered data processing instead. Not to mention a large bill for not much return? Maybe it's time you remembered your chief information officer, if you still have one.

The conventional wisdom today is that your technical people should properly be the champions of technology solutions to business problems. After all, they know it best. This should, however, be the very reason not to give them the keys to the car.

A love of technology for its own sake, however, is one of the reasons we have been landed with such a high learning cost for their programs. When was the last time someone asked for the fifty new features in an upgrade to their word processor?

Indeed, it is arguable that not only should the people who know most about technology not be its champions – they should in fact be its principal sceptics. After all, they surely know it well enough to understand what it can't do.

You perhaps can't see this happening because, amongst other things, the IT people themselves will resist any diminution in their role – no doubt attached to all kinds of dire warnings of pestilence which will befall you if you take away their discretionary budget. If so, you'd be right.

It won't be the CTO who makes this happen. In the past few years, the computer industry has congratulated itself that more and more companies are finding board seats for chief technology officers, but they shouldn't. Many companies may also be doing it to ensure they can keep an eye on the CTO and his growing budget, and also because they don't understand this stuff themselves, and don't want to hear second hand why it went wrong. Again.

The answer must surely lie in a renaissance for that much misunderstood, if not downright neglected, role of chief information officer.

Although it sounds like one of those made-for-Internet-TV job titles, CIOs actually pre-date CTOs, and – indeed – the modern computing era altogether.

They first emerged in the mid-1970s. When companies initially realized that information was too important to leave to chance, they began two processes. One was the digitization of knowledge, the path which has led us into the data processing age and the CTO. The other was the specialization of knowledge management, which gave us the CIO. Or not.

Here's some history, because it's important. In 1981, William Synott and William Gruber published *Information Resource Management: Opportunities and Strategies for the 1980s* (IRM). It documented, for the first time, the concept of IRM and the role it created for a senior executive – the CIO. Until the mid-1970s, companies had not really recognized that information was a strategic asset (or rather, they had forgotten that it was). Synott and

Gruber believed that CEOs thought this was way too important to leave to computer people to look after, and that they had created chief information officers to take control of the way their companies gathered and used information for strategic benefit.

The rise and fall of the CIO roughly then followed the changing fortunes of strategy and planning themselves through the 1980s and 1990s. In the heyday of strategic planning, when management writers such as Michael Porter were in the ascendant, the CIO role was strengthened. Managers placed a high value on strategic thinking, for which they needed a well-managed flow of information to them in order to make decisions.

Porter's most influential book, *Competitive Strategy* was itself published in 1980. It introduced the world to the five box schema (sounds exciting, even now). Within these five boxes, well informed managers would be able to assess their strategic options relative to expected responses and positions of competitors, potential entrants, buyers, suppliers and substitute markets. Porter introduced something he called the value chain to help companies understand their own competitive position. All of it based upon the use of information.

The role of the CIO flourished in this atmosphere, but went into decline with it, too. Strategy and planning have been somewhat out of fashion for much of the last decade. We've already looked at some of the forces which influenced this decline – most notably, the need for speed. If everything's happening so fast, and nothing can be predicted, why waste time on strategy?

So it was that the CIO position fell from favour, whilst the super-hyped technologists could dot com the corporation faster than you could say bull market and were valued accordingly – along with the computers and software they bought. You want evidence? Follow the money. According to a compensation survey by *Infoworld*, an industry publication, the average CIO salary in the US in 2001 was $110,697 in non-Internet companies. The average CTO salary in the same companies was nearly twice that: a whopping $203,759.

RISE AGAIN

Should the CIO rise again, the reason will most likely be as an antidote for a disillusion with technology investments made for their own sake and without any tangible return. Companies will have realised that return on

IT investment lies as much in the hands of the users as it does the programmers and the consultants who implement it. This can only be good. Indeed, the positive benefits are there for the taking, if only we allow ourselves to see them.

One observer who has thought as much about this as anyone is the academic Donald Marchand, who was one of the original students of the CIO professional. Marchand has been trying for over a decade now to alert companies to the fact that it's not what you know, but how you use it. Now, in 2002, he's begun to find companies who can still prove his point.

Marchand has studied, for example, the Cemex corporation of Mexico. Cemex makes cement – cue for a lame joke about new economy/old economy which will be avoided. However, this company has developed from a small commodity business to one of the three largest cement providers in the world. It has done so, Marchand argues, through having the correct attitude, or orientation, towards information in the business.

Cemex has invested large sums in satellite communications and GPS positioning. It knows, in near real time, exactly where every one of its trucks is, and has equally sophisticated systems feeding live data on production facilities into its HQ. Someone in Mexico is able to control the temperature of a kiln in Spain and can guarantee the delivery of ready-mix cement to its customers within a 20 minute window. Anyone who has had to wait at home for the plumber to come will know the frustration of not knowing quite when you will get service. Cemex clients are putting up buildings and making bridges. They can't wait: Cemex values information, Marchand says, so they don't have to.

Marchand's work[1] re-establishes the priority of information in the information technology equation, and it is unlikely that he will be a lone voice for much longer. Yes, Marchand has a nice, modern template for it: he speaks for example of managers having information capabilities to be able to see and act upon information which matters, and ignore data which doesn't.

Sometimes, though, things seem new not because they are, but because we have short memories and have forgotten something we shouldn't. Until the mid-1970s, when IT was invented, our companies had a much greater awareness of, and respect for, timely information. This was something which has always been true – before and since the apocryphal killing made by the Rothschilds at the battle of Waterloo. So we've had a decade or two

1 A useful summary paper by Marchand is available online from the European Business Foundation, ebfonline.com.

in which the technology mattered more than the information it conveyed. Time to turn the turtle back onto its belly.

SELF TEST: VICE OR VIRTUE?

Do you agree or disagree with the following statements:

1   IT infrastructure projects and desktop automation are the biggest contributors to productivity.
2   Small IT projects are of proportionately less value to the business as a whole than big projects.
3   Faster desktop systems with access to all relevant information have made each employee more productive, and therefore contributed to overall operating efficiency and better decisions.
4   Vendors of IT systems do genuinely have their customers interests at heart, and do a good job educating our technical people about the benefits of new ideas.
5   The chief technology officer should sit on the board not just because of the size of his budget but because decisions about which technologies to adopt are business-critical strategic issues.
6   The chief information officer is a secondary role whose position is simply to maximize the corporate use of the data which our technology produces, which is the right way round for productivity.

How did you score?

- If you agreed with all of the statements, you should cancel your subscription to *Wired* magazine and quit going to all those damned vendor conferences in Amsterdam. Start this chapter again.
- If you agreed with more than half of the statements, your life is not quite over, but you may have difficulties recognizing the difference between a good product that will help your business, and one which won't. Instead of trying to choose between vendors, ask if the new system is necessary at all.
- If you agreed with less than half of the statements, you border on the healthily sceptical, but be careful not to go too far. Sometimes an upgrade really is an upgrade, not a bug fix.

- If you didn't agree with any of the statements, you really need to get yourself a subscription to *Wired* magazine and start hanging out more with the technical people: your company needs you to know how to select the best tools available to do the job.

CHAPTER 9

Looking Good

I T IS NOT EASY TO KEEP YOUR CHILDREN ENTERTAINED on a wet Sunday in London, but if you're feeling environmentally minded and can get up early enough to beat the crowds, the Aquarium just next to Waterloo Station is a sure bet for a good time. It's also quite educational in some surprising ways. On a recent visit, for example, I noticed some illuminated notices had been installed as part of the Aquarium's quest to inform us all about diminishing fish populations due to over fishing.

It was next to a floor-to-ceiling shark tank and had one of those electronic tickers similar to the display in New York which counts up the US national debt. This one tells you how many tons of fish we've taken out of the sea and put on our plates so far this year. It was ticking along at a fair old clip, reflective of the increasing popularity of eating fish all round the world. In the US, for example, fish consumption reached 1.79 bn kilos in 1994. UK fish consumption is also increasing, by about 4% a year according to a very jolly Sea Fish Industry authority.

The information has, apparently, been put up to promote our awareness of the Marine Stewardship Council, an independent body based in London which is working towards sustainable harvesting of the seas. What a delicious irony, then, to discover the sponsor of this elaborate display: it is fish! plc, a swanky UK chain of fish restaurants.

This was, you might imagine, too good an invitation to turn down. As soon as midday arrived, my family and I decamped from the Aquarium to the nearest fish! establishment, where we could partake of a sustainable, deep fried, fish lunch. Happily, we did not have to go far for our treat. By fantastic coincidence, there happens to be a fish! diner just around the corner from the exhibit.

Inside, the paper menu cum placemat informs diners that 'at fish! we care about fish!'.[1] You better believe it. Their tuna are line-caught, the salmon organically reared, the langoustines retrieved from Loch Crinan without the need for trawling. Sadly, however, when one turns the page to the menu itself, of the 23 varieties of underwater flesh on offer, only one – mackerel – has the Marine Stewardship Council seal of approval. I think I had the cod. It was delicious.

Although far from being overcome by the guilt of knowingly contributing to the decline of the undersea population, I did find time later in the day to visit the Marine Stewardship Council website. Perhaps there were other restaurants where I could take my custom next time? There are indeed, but only if I can find another branch of fish!, which remains the only restaurant even to have one certified fish on the menu. Of course, I can always buy some Birds Eye Hoki fish fingers, to eat at home. They are made by Unilever, the company which set up the Marine Stewardship Council in 1997.

Corporations like fish! and Unilever want to be seen to be good citizens, but find it hard to be good businesses at the same time. As we shall see, there is a solution. You can be seen to try, to do the right thing, and hope that the thought counts enough. Hence, a corporate vice for looking good: an ethical fudge designed to take the political pressure off your business whilst you carry on regardless.

Most corporations would find, however, that business virtue is a better shield against their critics. What could be better for the world than highly efficient businesses which make the best use of resources – natural, human and intellectual?

NAUGHTY, NAUGHTY

You cannot blame corporations for their instinct to be seen to be doing something, anything, to take the pressure off from the many and varied environmental, social and ethical agendas now being hung around their necks. It is an act of self-defence.

Insurance is available for some of these third party risks, but by no means all of them. Actuaries will calculate risks for the unknown and accidents, but aren't much use for anything else. The insurable risk lexicon covers a multitude of sins, though: Asbestos, Bhopal, Chromium 6.[2]

But insurance has its limits. Once you get to tobacco the numbers are so large and the odds close enough to par that no Lloyds syndicate would

---

1 Just as well; Fish! plc went bust in July 2002.
2 The chemical pollutant discovered by Erin Brockovich.

come within a mile of the liability. There is also crime, and compensation suits for breach of contract. Just ask anyone who used to work for Arthur Andersen.

As most Andersen partners discovered to their cost, even the most lovingly cultivated corporate reputation is always a fragile thing. Loss of face is not an insurable risk either. The only cover you can get might be from a PR specialist, the people who can rebuild the public opinions of the oil companies over thirty or more years, or advise nuclear power stations to change their names and open visitor centres for kids to split the atom in 3D.

Mind you, some corporations clearly don't think the PR cover worth very much. One corporation was recently portrayed as seeking to avoid settling asbestos claims by declaring bankruptcy just before transferring the operating assets to a new entity and opening up down the road – free to trade without the baggage of dying ex-employees and their families. Who needs a reputation when you've got profits?

There is a further risk to corporate health which not only cannot be insured against, but often cannot be avoided without, literally, shutting up shop. I refer to the consumer boycotts, the fleeing investors, head banging politicians and nervous bankers of corporations who choose to do business in ways or places which offend public taste.

They took the scalp of Huntingdon Life Sciences when, in October 2001, the small drug testing company announced that it would relocate to the US from the UK, and list its shares on NASDAQ rather than in London. Huntingdon is a small lab, which was moderately profitable until a TV exposé in 1997 of the poor conditions in which it kept the animals used for testing. Ringed by placard bearers protesting against the cruelty within, its employees threatened at home on a regular enough basis to keep the company in the news, its shares fell from 116 pence to 3 pence as the company spent £20 m trying to stem a loss of customers. When the investors felt the heat of the protestors' threats, they backed off and left Huntingdon with no choice but to fold to fly.

GLOBALONEY

With trophies such as Huntingdon on their bookshelves, right next to those of a few tobacconists and more than one oil company, it's no wonder the agitators are feeling pleased with themselves. Some have gone so far as to declare, as John Gray has, that 'the era of globalization is over'. As such, we may well be about to enter a new phase in capitalism which authors such as John Elkington believe will make this the 'century of sustainable capitalism'. Are they right?

What is true is that globalization trends have been slowing down. During the 1990s, global trade grew by an average 7% each year; in the year 2000 it grew 12%, but there was an absolute standstill in 2001 and the expectation of an absolute decline in 2002. Capital flows also stalled: the UN reckons that foreign direct investment worldwide dropped 50% between 2000 and 2001 alone.

Look how capitalism is changing, they say. Markets and companies are embracing what Elkington calls the sustainability agenda which alters the dynamics of the economy, permanently. They could point out, for example, that since July 2000, UK pension funds have had to disclose whether or not they take account of citizenly concerns for the environmental, social and ethical impact of their investments. This, plus the good management of many so-called ethical funds, has produced a boom in the business of virtuous investing.

There are other signs that society is no longer going to tolerate the kind of misdemeanours highlighted by Elkington, Gray, Klein *et al*. Even their elected representatives have begun to pay attention. The US (but not the UK, yet) has long-standing legislation which seeks to prevent companies domiciled there from carrying out such nefarious acts overseas. Now they're using it, too.

In the first twenty years that this legislation existed, it was hardly exercised. This is not evidence that corporations were good, but that the authorities did not have the will or the means, to prosecute. There were less than two cases brought each year. But then in 2001 alone, the Securities and Exchange Commission settled three cases, and has more pending. One of those concluded involved $4.5 m in bribes paid by executives of IBM in Argentina to officials at a bank whose business it was pitching for.

From small acorns: no doubt the SEC hoped that the massive fine of $300,000 which IBM was ordered to pay was as nothing compared to the damage which had been done to its reputation by this scandal. But then no one realized at the time that Argentina itself would go bust less than a year later. In any event, multinational corporations which are still very much alive, and kicking those they shouldn't be, may do well to watch their backs.

All this might indicate that business has, finally, learnt how to accommodate its wider social responsibility within business virtue. But if you look a little closer at what corporations are actually doing, it is not business virtue that they have extended, but a corporate vice for looking good, whilst still doing bad.

THREE LINE WHIP

The apparent transformation of business virtue from naked self-interest to enlightened common benefit comes down in large part to a neat little accounting concept called the Triple Bottom Line. In *Cannibals With Forks*, John Elkington describes the Triple Bottom Line as a way of accounting for 'economic prosperity, environmental quality, and – the element which business has preferred to overlook – social justice'. The Triple Bottom line is the intellectual and moral underpinning for corporate citizenship.

The Triple Bottom Line, simply put, places alongside the financial bottom line both environmental and social accounts. Appearing – often literally – in the accounts, both are expressed in terms of the use, and return on, capital. The definition of capital is much wider than the assets you learnt about in school; it includes other people's assets and common resources (like water and air) as well as social capital. This formula allows companies an acceptable way to express the greater good in terms they are very familiar with – financial self-interest.

The Triple Bottom Line is catching on with corporations and their customers. In early February 2002, the chief executives of 36 of the world's largest companies – including McDonalds and Coca-Cola – signed up to a common pledge on corporate citizenship. All the usual virtues are there, including environmental concern, respect for various species, sustainability etc. How serious are they?

For example, one of the signatories to that convention, the German engineering company Siemens, already issues an annual report on its own efforts at corporate citizenship. The CEO wants you to know that 'corporate citizenship is our global commitment ... we are committed to protecting our environment', and that 'cultural differences enrich our organization'. Fine words, too – but there is more to it than that.

Siemens has also, since 2000, been listed in the Dow Jones Sustainability Index – a group of ethically concerned corporations who now have a UK equivalent in the even more select FTSE4Good Index. The DJSI lets in companies which it assesses meet stringent criteria for what it calls 'corporate sustainability', defined as 'a business approach that creates long-term shareholder value by embracing opportunities and managing risks deriving from economic, environmental and social developments'. Thanks to the Triple Bottom Line, even the Dow Jones has adapted to the citizenship agenda.

It's not just the companies themselves that like the Triple Bottom Line formula. Customers and investors like it too.

It used to be that ethical investing was little more than a worthwhile way to lose money. Until the UK government went out of its way to require every pension fund to declare its citizenly credentials, ethical funds were a niche business with underwhelming returns. 6% of British investors reported in an NOP survey early in 2002 that they favoured ethical funds, and some good financial performance has helped grow the sector: it now accounts for 5% of all funds under management in the UK and 13% in the US. So can it pay to be good?

One company which believes that corporate citizenship is good for business is an old hand at the game. Novo Nordisk, a European pharmaceuticals company, has been following the Triple Bottom Line since the early 1990s. As well being a good citizen, Novo Nordisk was rated one of the top ten European companies in a 2002 *Forbes Magazine* survey, and consistently turns in upper quartile sector returns and outperforms its peers in creating shareholder value.

How do they do it? Almost certainly, Novo Nordisk benefits from not giving its people a choice. Targets relating to the other two bottom lines are set, and enforced, alongside those like sales, margins and quality control which directly influence the original bottom line. For example, business units in the company are expected to increase energy and water efficiency by up to 5% each year.

The social bottom line is probably the hardest of the three to measure. How do you count virtue? Novo Nordisk sets some internal targets, like reducing workplace injuries, which are obviously related to the financial bottom line and should be uncontroversial. But it also engages in doing good, rather than just avoiding harm. A large part of Novo Nordisk's business, for example, is the treatment of diabetes. It sets as one of its social responsibility goals the development, in the words of its vice president for ethics and responsibility, of 'a sustainable business model for helping people with diabetes in poor countries to gain access to health care'.

As well as making these objectives mandatory, Novo Nordisk treats them as they would any financial goal. Failure is reflected in bonus calculations, and can hit your career prospects too. Every few years, a team of seventeen senior executives can be expected to descend on each business unit and crawl all over it in an extensive environmental audit. Their findings make it to the board. Oh, and they pay the accountants DeLoitte & Touche to check all their calculations.

WHO DO THEY THINK THEY'RE KIDDING?

Is it all for real? Is the Triple Bottom Line really changing business virtue, as its promoters hope, or is it being manipulated by corporations less interested in business virtue than needing to evade the pressures of the eco-lobby?

The balance of evidence suggests the latter. A closer look at the way some equity markets have recognized the triple bottom line suggests more style than substance. The Dow Jones Sustainability Index has, for example, three criteria – economic, environmental and social – by which to measure a sustainably managed corporation. They are detailed and entirely in line with the Triple Bottom Line agenda. They're also errant nonsense.

Take the top line, economic criteria. It includes productivity measures like IT investment (ha ha), risk management and crisis management. As companies exist to generate productivity, there is nothing special to be found here. A good business is one which gets the most out of the least resources. End of story. Get yourself into the DJSI, however, and at least your computers will tell you when your oil tanker has ruptured, and a press release will be on hand to help mitigate the damage it may cause to your credentials. In short: the index doesn't measure how wasteful you are, just how efficient you are at it.

There are equally absurd possibilities in the rest of the DJSI criteria. The middle line, environment, gives highest marks to corporations that have good environmental performance (4 points), but even if you don't you can still get in by having a nice looking environmental charter (3.8 points), policy (3 points) and an appointee, like Mr Jennings of Novo Nordisk, to promote your citizenly credentials (2.6 points). Yes, a company which pollutes every river it draws from but worries about it in public, is just as good as one which never harmed a butterfly and conserves as much energy as possible.

Then there's the last line, social responsibility. We already know that this is the hardest to develop robust measures for, and it should be no surprise that this set of criteria are the strangest. A DJSI listed company gets top marks (4.5) for having stakeholder involvement, whatever that means.

There are equal marks (3 each) for having someone responsible for social policy and equitable remuneration. This is just as well, for corporations can only expect one point each for allowing free association, furthering the cause of equal rights, and demonstrating high levels of employee satisfaction. If only you could talk your way to social responsibility.

It would be a fairly naïve person who would consider this a great step forward for capitalism. Most of the words suitable to describe it should not appear in respectable business books like this one. It would be hard not to argue that corporations have decided that the best way to get the environmentalists off their backs is to appease them: for example, joining indices like FTSE4Good and the DJSI, with their low-impact ethical commitments. Even Vernon Jennings, the man in charge of making sure that Novo Nordisk behaves itself, confessed recently that the market out-performance of the DJSI companies 'could be interpreted as merely proving that only successful companies can afford to pursue the Triple Bottom Line'.

UNSUSTAINABLE ARGUMENTS

So, many of these apparently ethically minded, responsible corporations may really be taking us all for a ride. One person who thinks so is the economist David Henderson. In 2001, Henderson blew the whistle on the good citizens of the corporate world by exposing the nonsense of what he called 'global salvationism' – 'a belief that fateful choices have to be made on behalf of humanity and the planet, and a distorted view of globalisation and its effects'.

I simplify a subtle argument, but his view is that by making businesses less productive, less business virtuous, less efficient in their use of the world's resources, less effective in allocating capital to where it is best used, these well meaning agendas would only harm their causes. Worse still, by forcing companies and markets to operate against their natural instincts would only encourage cheating.

There are good reasons to think that David Henderson is onto something. Take one irregular market intervention into the UK energy market through the Government's introduction in April 2001 of the climate change levy. This well intentioned tax aims to reduce demand for energy by British companies in two ways. First, it levies an additional charge on consumption – a number of pence per kilowatt hour of electricity or gas, and so on. The tax is almost neutralized overall by a drop in employment tax, but leaves

£120 m spare to promote the energy efficiency to companies. The hope is to produce a market which values energy efficiency faster than would happen normally, if at all.

The experience of the first year of this exercise suggests it isn't likely to work. Those corporations which are heavy energy consumers, and have agreed to attempt to meet existing efficiency targets created by government get an 80% discount on the levy. Lucky them. Small businesses are not so well placed. The market has not provided them with the chance to buy energy supplies from renewable sources which would be exempt from the levy. Nor do they have the cash flow necessary to make the investment in extra efficiency that would reduce the impact. They'll just have to absorb the extra costs, keep consuming power at no benefit to the environment. This is the kind of net loss which Mr Henderson predicted.

Then there are the social welfare considerations of the Triple Bottom Line to consider. Involvement here by governments can, Henderson says, 'undermine freedom of contract and thus deprive people of opportunities'. His argument is weaker here. Some involvement in freedom of contract – like restricting the use of child labour – is both valuable to society and creates opportunity. In one respect, however, he is right.

There is a further side-effect of the institutionalization of good citizenship which is even more disturbing. Many companies pursuing the agenda of corporate responsibility have stopped giving money to charity and local community projects, now that they have global market programs to contend with. Last year, business contributed less than 5% of the voluntary sector's income of £15.6 bn – almost half what it gave a decade before.

They are not complete misers, though, particularly when it comes to spending other people's time for them. Many now warmly request their staff to go out into the community to do good works in the name of the corporation. They often also insist that this time is taken outside of work and, speaking to many of these volunteers, it is clear that social pressure accounts for a lot of the take-up in many such projects.

Not only do corporations with a vice for looking good use measures like Triple Bottom Line to evade their responsibilities, but this is not in the interests of business virtue.

IT'S STILL PRODUCTIVITY

If productivity is the best a corporation can do for the world, maybe there is no need for the institutions and market mechanisms which the promoters of sustainable capitalism want to set up. In fact, they may – as David Henderson believes – be antithetical to the very thing which we need most: business virtue.

Support for this argument comes from some unlikely sources. In a book published in April 2002, the scientist Edmund O. Wilson has made and maintained a strong case for sustainable economics. Wilson argues, however, that globalization and innovation are the very forces which are causing world-saving changes, like the decline in population growth – as well as socially-improving trends like the education and empowerment of women.

He points out, however, that projections of doom will still hold unless mankind opens some 'escape hatches'. One such would be clean, renewable energy that would release us from our dependence upon fossil fuels. He's right. If you believe in the market, then you'll believe that competition, and the profit motive, is still the best way to ensure this happens. No government, institution, regulator or trading scheme has ever proven itself wiser, faster, or more sustainable than a properly functioning market. You just can't do better than business virtue.

SELF TEST: VICE OR VIRTUE?

Do you agree or disagree with the following statements:

1   Most corporations have a wider social, environmental and moral responsibility than their commercial needs might recognize, but which are equally important to their viability as businesses in the long run.
2   Not all commercial risks are insurable; some cannot even be quantified but this should not prevent companies from finding ways to incorporate social costs into the balance sheet.
3   Those companies contributing the most to a sustainable environment are not necessarily the most efficient, but those that follow the Triple Bottom Line accounting principles.
4   Membership of indices such as FTSE4Good and the Dow Jones Sustainability Index is reliable sign that a company has really taken environment and social concerns on board and is doing something positive.

5   The traditional means by which companies engaged with the community, such as charitable giving, are in decline because corporations are able to give something back in other, more valuable ways recognized as global standards like the Triple Bottom Line.

6   Free trade and efficient corporations are less likely to deliver better use of the world's resources than would a definitive global regulatory regime.

How did you score?

- If you agreed with all of the statements, have you recently come across *No Logo* or *Captive State* by any chance? Do you think your company might sponsor you to go protest at Davos next year?
- If you agreed with more than half of the statements, you have perhaps too rosy a view of the interaction between corporations and environmental economics.
- If you agreed with less than half of the statements, you have a sceptical view of the response of corporations to environmental concerns, and devices like Triple Bottom Line. Don't let it go too far: sometimes, the fish really are depleted.
- If you did not agree with any of the statements, you really ought to read *No Logo*. Sometimes, business virtue is not all it seems to be either

CHAPTER 10

Better Times

L URKING SOMEWHERE WITHIN THE BRITISH MUSEUM is an intellectual sar- cophagus: a seven-foot-high by five-foot-wide replica of an early type of computer designed to model the workings of the economy using nothing more sophisticated than plumbing. The original machine was built in 1949 at the London School of Economics by Bill Phillips, an engineer from New Zealand who thought he could use coloured liquids running along Perspex tubes and rubber hoses to make flesh the rules and variables of economic forces as they were then understood. Two students would be employed to operate it, opening valves and pumping through them liquids representative of money, jobs, prices and so on. Profits rose, water levels fell. Bill was justifiably proud of his machine. He reckoned it produced an error of just 4%.

Sadly, should you wish to pay homage to the device, you will find the British Museum's version out of order at this time. This is probably quite fitting. It's been a few years since anyone would have admitted to believing that Bill Phillips' machine could ever have really been able to model a com- plex economic world in such a crude but accurate way. Instead, we've been gorging ourselves on the wilder shores of chaos theory, where a butterfly in Caracas can cause a collapse on the NASDAQ, or floating ever upwards in a parallel universe where the business cycle has been abolished.

It's a pity more business people cannot see the appeal of a slightly less exotic, even volatile, taste in economic fashions. What's wrong with thinking the world might actually be as set in its ways as Bill Phillips' tubes? At 4%, his margin for error was, after all, considerably more attrac- tive than a theory which would give equal odds of a new depression every other Thursday. Anyone who did think so would almost certainly be less inclined to the corporate vice of over-reacting to changes in the economic weather.

The fact is that recessions are never pretty, but perhaps as much as half the damage they do is self-inflicted – not by governments trying to fix the economy, but by corporations trying to fix themselves. Each major downturn in the UK since 1918, for example, has taken a 10% average bite out of the economy. Half of that wealth was permanently lost to us.

Over-reacting to the downward part of the business cycle is a chronic corporate vice that has cost us all dear. After four major recessions and several close calls since the end of WWI, by the start of 2003 we will be about a third poorer than we would have been had corporations not gone too far in their remedies for the problems they faced, or left themselves so vulnerable to damage in the first place.

NORMALCY

The story we tell our children, and ourselves, about most recessions is that they're either someone else's fault or just a ghastly mistake. Bad things don't just happen to good economies and businesses. Heroic finance ministers or clever economists come to our rescue from evil villains, and before you know it we're off again. It's mostly nonsense, but it does make us feel better – normally before turning a further notch of credit.

It could be the OPEC ministers we blame, for example. They're the nasty people who caused the two longest recessions in the past 50 years by hiking their prices without notice. Or it could be your own government to blame. Those morons who, say, went for the gold standard (or abandoned it), furthered free trade (or didn't), lowered interest rates (or raised them), spent too much (or too little).

It's fair, in one way, to think of recessions as accidents that cause temporary interruptions in the normal economic service of growth and corporate wealth creation. Even by the most widely accepted definition that a recession is two successive quarters in which an economy got smaller, Britain has experienced only four major recessions since 1918. Together, they spanned sixteen years. That's roughly one year of recession for every five years of growth – not bad going at all.

Recently, however, people began to wonder if these little accidents might not be preventable altogether. It caught on, to the point where people with no idea what they were talking about could hold a solid conversation about the new economy with their bank manager, often in the hope of being able to borrow more money to invest on the wonder stocks like Cisco and Microsoft which were ushering in a new age of permanent prosperity.

The whole end of economic cycles thing started in 1997 – with only five years of normal service out of the 1989–92 recession. Steven Weber, a professor of political science at the University of California at Berkeley, wrote an article in the musty journal, *Foreign Affairs*, entitled 'The End of the Business Cycle?' A good place for heresy: it was *Foreign Affairs* which published, anonymously, the article which first articulated the US Cold War strategy of containment which prepared the way for events like the Vietnam war and today's policy toward Taiwan. Weber's article was to have a similar impact in the world of business and economics.

Having confessed that 'no one is sure why business cycles occur', Weber did not argue that there would never be another depression (he isn't stupid). But he did think that downturns would now be less frequent, and less deep, than previously. Even the unpredictable potential damage inflicted by big economic surprises from outside (like OPEC hiking the oil price) should largely be within our control from now on.

ANATOMY OF A BOOM

With such exciting a prospect as permanent upswings, corporations displayed their awesome powers of over-reaction to economic news by feeding their cash flow into the afterburners. In a few years, companies like Marconi have consumed the billions they had in reserve, carefully accumulated from years of steady growth, and found themselves on the verge of bankruptcy with a credit rating worse than Delorean. Others, such as WorldCom, have appeared from nowhere to become amongst the most highly valued companies in the world, only to disappear as quickly when the music stopped.

You can, in fact, put quite a precise date on it. In July 1997, the same month that Weber's paper was published, *Wired* magazine published a breathless article by Peters Schwarz and Leyden entitled 'The Long Boom: A History of the Future'.

The authors could hardly contain themselves: 'we are riding the early waves', they said, 'of a 25-year run of a greatly expanding economy that will do much to solve seemingly intractable problems like poverty and to ease tensions throughout the world'. Wealth and world peace. How? Simple: 'two metatrends – fundamental technological change and a new ethos of openness – will transform our world into the beginnings of a global civilization, a new civilization of civilizations, that will blossom through the coming century'. *Wired* readers wrote to the editor about how they cried when they read this, so overwhelmed were they by the certainty of endless, unlimited wealth creation.

It was nonsense then, and it's nonsense now, not that anyone was listening to the few dissenting voices. When the tide is rising, in President Kennedy's memorable homily, all the boats float upwards. He didn't need to add that those which don't are sinking.

Even for a committed optimist, 1997 was very early in the upswing to declare victory over the business cycle. We had experienced about five years of growth at this point – an average cyclical upswing. The record still stands at 28 years, the period of almost uninterrupted growth experienced by the UK and US economies between 1945 and 1973. Anyone suggesting the business cycle was dead during this period was laughed at openly.

At about 3% a year, the 1992–1997 growth rate hadn't exactly been an Olympic feat, either. Between 1992 and 1996, the UK economy had expanded a very average 2.7% a year. The US was growing faster, but again not markedly above its previous high scores. And it had not yet caught up the ground lost in the downturn.

It would be a complete mystery why the corporate world went growth crazy in the spring of 1997 if it weren't for the panegyrics of Weber, Schwarz, Leyden and everyone working for ZDTV, *Business 2.0* and the *Industry Standard* towards all things Internet. This technology was giving business a productivity boost which was unprecedented and blew away our feeble expectations of return on capital. The IT was also making markets super efficient and removing the dangers of over stocking, price volatility and other brakes on sustained growth. Hence, a new economy.

It became even harder to resist in the follow year as growth continued and accelerated into the stock market boom of 1999. Every measure of activity was in overdrive. Mergers and acquisitions, as we have seen, moved trillions of dollars around the economy – much of it funded by debt or paid for with shares. Real wages grew at almost unprecedented rates, eating into company profits. People needed the money, though: the property market in San Francisco, for example, made overnight millionaires out of grannies with two bed condos. By 1999, even Alan Greenspan was talking up the apparent productivity miracle in the US: official figures showed an annual increase over 4% in 2000 alone. Why stop there?

OOPS, A DOWNTURN

If business over-reacted to the promise of a prolonged boom, and created a speculative bubble from debt and deception, that was nothing compared to what came next. For the corporate over-reaction to the downturn of 2001 will almost certainly have as many ill effects on our businesses for years to come, even after normal economic service has resumed.

When the turn came, it was less than expected: it felt and looked like betrayal. For a while, many people even refused to believe it was happening. They had entirely missed the signs which usually presaged a downturn in the offing – such as falling car sales and a decline in house building, rising corporate debt and too-high levels of stock building up in warehouses.

However, it was also clear at the time that many of the fundamentals which support real economic growth remained sound. There was no spike in inflation or overflowing money supply to cause concern. Unemployment rates in most developed countries were low but not invisible, meaning that an adjustment may occur to real wages but not enough to cause lasting pain. The prices of other major assets in the economy, particularly housing, were robust and not overly geared. And electorates the world over were renewing the terms in office of their governments, a sure sign of satisfaction with their economic stewardship.

But still corporations found the evidence they needed to over-react. Markets had turned. By the end of May 2001 a total of over $3 trn had been destroyed on the US stock markets alone. A further $4 trn disappeared from London, Frankfurt, Paris, Hong Kong, and elsewhere. NASDAQ, the easy-in tech-heavy market in which many of the dot com placements had occurred, lost over 60% of its value; many stocks lost over 90% of their worth in a matter of weeks.

For those looking for evidence that this was, indeed, the end of the world, plenty of omens were available. Globalization of trade, only yesterday the engine of growth, today meant that America's suppliers and its customers fully expected to be sucked down with it. Those who had happily taken inward investment from US companies and banks suddenly worried that they may pull out: it must surely be easier to fire workers in a Welsh town than in your home town. Those who had lent money to fund voracious corporate expansion in the US feared they would never see their cash again. They were mostly right, too.

To add to the agony, many of those trillions which evaporated from the world's stock markets represented the savings and loans of ordinary people to a greater extent than in any previous such collapse. Half of all American and a quarter of UK households now own the shares whose value tumbled by two thirds. Before anyone says they only have themselves to blame, it is worth recalling that this was the result of long-term changes in capital markets which made equities a smart investment choice. Between 1991 and 2000, the average return on equities was 14% a year – twice that of boring old government bonds, whilst in the previous decade, bonds were a better place to put your money than shares – and we did.

With a vice for over-reacting to economic news, with so many apparently good reasons to panic, it's no surprise that this is exactly what corporations did.

QUICK, PANIC

Once they start on it, corporations do tend to panic in some very predictable ways.

Apparently, the first rule of good management when a recession occurs is to give yourself a really good beating. According to research by the National Institute of Economic and Social Research, over 50% of UK companies consider 'focus on the core business' an important step to survival. What this means is pain, and lots of it. Over 45% consider their focusing to include reducing their workforce as much as necessary, and a third would reduce inventories to the lowest level consistent with scraping the bottom.

The thing to do is to take a really big knife and start cutting. Of course, there are always corporations that cannot survive the dose of pain felt necessary. Many companies which were already dicey – venture funded, loss making, new starters (including my own) – simply folded or were sold at bargain basement prices as the prospect of future investment, and revenues, went away. Those plucky entrepreneurs who put up a fight mostly ended up having their passports confiscated by the bankruptcy court.

No business is, of course, ever harmed by being more productive, and a lot of emergency belt-tightening can be virtuous. Too much, however, might not be. This doesn't mean they don't often meet their purpose. Those cuts to productive business assets which cause more damage than is strictly necessary in business terms may have a very compelling corporation logic – particularly if the point is to save the management's own skin.

MEA CULPA, MEA MAXIMA CULPA

In a recession, unfortunately, it often pays managers to do unnecessarily bad things to their business for the sake of their corporate lives. The market expects it, and generally rewards those with the sharpest knives making the deepest cuts, irrespective of business virtue.

To see just how to observe the first principle of recession management, look no further than the actions of one past masters of the art: the Ford Motor Company – a century old, and one of the world's largest auto manufacturers. They've seen off a few recessions in their time, and this is no exception.

Since 2000, auto makers worldwide have faced not just unprecedented falls in demand in major markets, such as the US, but also brutal price competition and volatile raw material costs. The news just kept getting worse. As late as February 2002, Ford was reporting car sales down 12% in the US compared to the year before.

After first sacking its still popular but now sacrificial CEO lamb, Ford managed to administer most of its self-inflicted agony in one go. In January 2002, it announced that losses for 2001 had come in at a withering – but not unexpected – $5.4 bn worldwide. And with these figures came the curative. It was a very big pill.

Mea culpa: 35,000 job cuts worldwide and the closure of five North American plants. Mea maxima culpa: Ford described the cost cutting as a strategic restructuring which promised to give investors $9 bn of additional revenues by 2005. It's hard to imagine a bigger pill, but Ford executives set off an a road show around the world's financial capitals to tell investors how great this plan was and why they should believe it.

With favourable reviews, and all the credibility they needed, did Ford's slice and dice management suffer a horrible run on its stock price? Not at all. It was a quiet day on the Ford ticker: analysts confirmed the market sentiment that the company had done enough to retain the confidence of investors. The managers had made it through. Hurrah for the managers.

This may seem perverse behaviour on the part of the markets, but no one can accuse them of being inconsistent in their application of this strange logic. Whilst rewarding corporations like Ford which play the game, they reserve some nasty punishments for those who don't – even when they are clearly acting in the best interest of the business and its shareholders.

One such miscreant recently was the network equipment company Cisco. In May 2001 it announced that is was going to destroy $2.25 bn of unsold stock. Just like that. No sackings, no apology, no real explanation. One Wall Street analyst commented acidly that 'What everyone is missing here is that Cisco's inventory is not the problem, but a symptom,' he said. 'A company that has been preaching to the choir about the capacity of its management has proven it isn't perfect. Good management doesn't wind up with a ($2.2 bn) inventory write-off'. As a punishment, the stock market took 6% off Cisco's market capitalization that day, and a lot more off the goodwill it may be prepared to extend to its executives in future.

The first rule of recession management – to cut until after it hurts – really has a lot to answer for. It inspires the self-mutilation of businesses far beyond what is virtuous. If this happens enough – too many companies taking too much out of their operations and retreating too far from innovation, investment and expansion – the downturn can quickly become a permanent economic setback.

The record suggests it normally does, too. One way to measure this is in the gap between where we are now and where we would have been had the recessions of the past not happened. In his book, *Major Recessions*, the economist Christopher Dow calculated that even in 1993 – just after the last recession – UK output was as much as 25% below where it would have been had growth not been interrupted by the recessions of 1973, 1979 and 1989. Across the whole of the last century, he reckons that a typical recession reduces the size of the economy by about 10%, of which about half is recovered in the upswing, but half is lost for good.

None of this is, however, necessary.

A MORE VIRTUOUS WAY TO SEE THINGS

Your average recession is very over-rated as a significant economic event. In fact, most of what actually matters to business success or failure doesn't materially change in a recession, or indeed at any point in the economic cycle. What matters, of course, is business virtue.

Those companies which fail in bad times are generally the same as those which fail in good times, and those which make it do so whatever the weather. Take the present situation in the world's large commercial airlines. As many column inches have been given in the business press to no-frills airlines who have been taking on employees just as to the bigger carriers who have been laying them off.

Why is this news? The big guys have been losing billions and firing thousands; the upstarts – like EasyJet and RyanAir in the UK, or Southwest in the US – have taken on a few hundred and made a few million. At any other time, the growth of the no-frills would be likely to get attention in the corner of the page reserved for novelty items or small business news.

Whatever point we're at in the business cycle, if you're going to fail, you're going to fail. Swissair, for example, was a basket case long before September 11th. Following the suggestion of McKinsey a year or so earlier, Swissair management had blown $1 bn on stakes in other small European airlines with whom it wanted to partner. By July 2001, its debts were six times the value of the company. It's hard to see how this company could have held it together, even in a boom.

And if you're going to succeed, you will anyway – regardless of the ups and downs of the world at large. Southwest, EasyJet and Ryanair have done well in the recession, but they were doing just as well, if not more so, before. In the automobile industry, where companies like Ford have experienced perilous drops in sales, others – such as BMW – have been able to maintain and even accelerate growth. In 2001, it increased profits by 60% and increased its sales in the US despite shrinkage in the market overall.

You can hardly put BMW, a European maker of expensive executive cars, in the same basket as no-frills airlines. Cheap and cheerful is not a word one associates with a £30,000 plus urban assault vehicle like the X5 SUV. Nor can you generalize the opposite, that people will always pay for quality: the 2000–2002 downturn has been a particularly torrid time for luxury goods makers in general. In his statement announcing the 2001 figures, BMW's chief executive simply didn't need to talk about the economic climate. He had products and productivity to report. In other words, BMW is a well managed business – whatever the weather.

THE REAL DEAL

It's also worth stopping by on our way to the upswing to point out that companies which think the recovery will save them are just as likely to fall on their faces when things get better. And for the same reasons.

Yes, rising demand obscures all kinds of corporate vices, mostly of the wastage variety. Yes, the prospect of growth also tends to buoy stock prices artificially and bring new venture capital in to fund riskier enterprises. No, it still doesn't mean that the basic rules of good or bad management ever change. Business virtue is not a cyclical requirement, but a permanent one.

A study by the Bank of England in 2001 showed that, for the UK at least, the factors which push companies over the edge may even run counter to the economic cycle – actually increasing vulnerability in good times.

Take start-ups. The Bank of England points out that the failure rate of new businesses is always high, and warns not to read too much into this: particularly good advice for anyone who suffered in the NASDAQ meltdown, where you could get a listing almost as soon as the ink was dry on your incorporation. They're right: during an upswing, business creation does tend to rise as risk aversion drops and capital is easier to find. So does the failure rate, but this is a trick of the numbers. The same high proportion of start-ups is failing within the first couple of years – at any point in the cycle, there are just more of them in a boom.

The Bank of England's careful analysis shows that corporate failure rates are not linked mainly to things we only associate with recession. In fact, the opposite in many cases.

Real interest rates, for example, have a direct impact on solvency, since firms can't meet their loan payments when rates rise faster than prices. But, as we have seen in the past couple of years, interest rates don't always rise in recessions. In fact, they tend to do so now in good times – when central banks are trying to cool down an overheated economy.

Wage demands are also a big factor, unsurprisingly, because of the immediate impact they have on productivity, cash flow and productivity. Rising real wages in the economy between 1988 and 1992 accounted for 43% of the increase in bankruptcies. Yet the conventional wisdom is that workers are afraid to press for higher wages when a recession is on – high unemployment means your employer may be less afraid of getting rid of you if a replacement is already waiting in line. The lesson: real wage rises can hurt you, at any time.

It all serves to reinforce the sorry truth that recessions wouldn't be half as bad for us if we didn't go twice as crazy as we needed to when one comes along. Accidents do happen, but some of us have insurance. It's called productivity, the basic discipline of a virtuous business. Stick with it and you can't go far wrong.

SELF TEST: VICE OR VIRTUE?

Do you agree or disagree with the following statements:

1   Recessions needn't happen; they are avoidable malfunctions of the economy, and temporary interruptions to the normal pattern of growth.
2   Every company should take maximum advantage of periods of economic growth by maximizing its market share by whatever financial and strategic means necessary.
3   The new economy is based upon the power of technology to permanently remove inefficiency from the market, meaning that old limits on growth and productivity simply have no relevance any more.
4   The first duty of a corporation when a downswing occurs is to protect itself, which means making whatever painful cuts are necessary to retain market confidence in the management team.
5   Once a corporation has made the necessary cuts to ensure survival, the best strategy is to wait out the downswing until growth resumes. Then the company can build itself up again and take full advantage of those growth opportunities as before.
6   Corporations which go to the wall in a recession can't be blamed for bad economic conditions, but those which succeed during an upswing can take the credit for their achievement.

How did you do?

- If you agreed with all of the statements, you obviously haven't been paying much attention. Do you drive a new Beetle and hang out at new economy networking evenings on the first Tuesday of each month?
- If you agreed with more than half of the statements, you are probably at risk of losing any business virtue you acquired, even by default, in this downturn. Try not to if you don't want to go through the last eighteen months again next time.

- If you agreed with less than half of the statements, you are likely to have taken on board the point that business virtue is not an optional extra; by keeping your discipline at any point of the cycle, your business will have the best chance of success.
- If you agreed with none of the statements, you really need to get out more. You're in danger of either missing every opportunity, or of always calling it wrong. Go smell the Martinis at a first Tuesday near you sometime.

Index

Accenture 78
accounts
  audited 12–13, 15
  cooking the books 14–15
  pro forma 12–13, 15
  rules/regulations 15–16
acquisitions *see* mergers and
    acquisitions
advertising 8, 60–1
  agency system 64–6
  branding activity 66–9
  sales/marketing relationship
    69–70
  success 62–4
agency problem 25–6
airline companies 127
alliances 78–80
Allied Domecq 41
Amazon.com 74, 77
Arthur Andersen 110
artificial markets 85–7
Asda 49–50, 51, 55
AT&T 79–80

balance sheets 12–14
Bank of England 128
Barney deals 78–80
Bernstein, Peter 84
Bezos, Jeff 77
BhS 45
Bland, Sir Christopher 44
Bloomer, Jonathan 25
BMW 127

Bonfield, Sir Peter 44
Booz-Allen & Hamilton 79
Breen, Peter 39
Bristol-Myers Squibb 63–4, 69
British Museum 119
British Telecom (BT) 28, 44, 79–80, 90
BSkyB 76, 77
Buffett, Warren 30
Burger King (UK) 51
business cycles
  boom 121–2
  recession 119–21, 123–9
business fundamentals
  different views 16–18
  productivity 18–19, 22

Campbell Soup 41
CAP Gemini 102
capital relations
  good 30–1
  investors 29–30
  legislation 28–9
  ownership 29–30
capitalism 2–7, 111
carve-outs 32, 34
Cemex corporation 105
Cendant corporation 14–15
chaos theory 119
Chiat, Jay 65
chief information office (CIO) 102
  decline 104
  emergence 103–4
  rise 105

chief technology officer (CTO) 102,
103, 104
CIO Magazine 99, 101
Cisco Systems 11–12, 73, 76, 121, 126
Clarinex 63
Claritin 63, 64
Coase, Ronald 20–1
Coca-Cola 76, 85, 112
competition 71–5
ConArgra Food 41
Concert 79–80
Cone, Fairfax 62
corporate citizenship 112–15
corporations
  confidence in 6–7
  decline 5–6
  dysfunctional methods of hiring/
    firing 44–5
  golden age 4–5
  growth 3–4
  new types 6
  ownership 29
  recruitment/payment of talent 36–47
  vices 8–9
  virtues 2, 7
cost control 18, 19
Courtney, Hugh 88
Crain, Rance 61
Crawford, Philip 42
CUC International 14
Customer Relationship Management
  (CRM) 95, 99–100
customers 75–8

data processing 97–8
Davies, Michael 48–9, 52
De Lorean, John 22
decision-making 1–2, 27
Dell computer 98
Diet Coke 76
Dow, Christopher 126
Dow Jones Sustainability Index (DJSI)
  112–13, 114, 115
Drucker, Peter 4–5, 39
Dunnhumby 85

EasyJet 127
eBay 76
Ebbers, Bernie 71, 73, 74
EDS 32, 42
Elkington, John 111, 112
employees 27–8
Enron 28
environmental accounting 9, 112, 113,
  114, 115–16
ethics 9, 109, 111, 115
executives
  caveat emptor 46–7
  demand and supply 39–40
  effective compensation 45
  exit interviews 36–7
  finding new jobs 42–3
  golden handshakes 43–4
  headhunting 38–9
  loss of job 36–7
  pay/rewards 37–8, 41
  personal investment 45–6
  price of 39–40
  quality fall/price rise 41–2
  removing 42–4
  secrecy on departure 43
  share options 45–6
  talent 38–40
  time in job 42
  volatility of position 42
  wage inflation 40–1

fashion industry 91
Ferguson, Niall 95
first mover advantage 76–7
fish! plc 109
Food and Drugs Administration (FDA)
  62
Ford Motor Company 21, 55, 58, 125
Foreign Affairs journal 121
Foresight Exchange 86
FTSE4Good Index 112, 115
Futurebrand 67
futurology 9
  artificial market technique 86–7
  Business Class/Prism scenarios 82–3

cyclical 83–4
games theory 87–90
myopia of prediction 91–2
probability/sampling 84–5

3G mobiles 89–90
Gallup 50, 85
games theory
    auction process 89–90
    in practice 87–9
    prisoner's dilemma 89
Gartner Group 99
General Electric (GE) 74
General Motors (GM) 32
Gent, Chris 45, 72
Gibbons, Barry 51
Glaxo SmithKline 66–7
Glaxo Wellcome 67
globalization 110–11, 123
Goldman Sachs 34
Gore, Al 63
Gray, John 110
Green, Philip 45–6
Greenberg, Jack 57
Greenspan, Alan 122
Gruber, William 103–4
Gucci 29

Haagen Dazs 76
Halewood (Merseyside) 21, 22
Hammer, Michael 6
Handy, Charles 6, 39
Heidrick and Struggles 39
Heineken 33, 74
Henderson, David 115, 117
HFS Inc 14
Hollywood stock exchange 86, 87
Honda 68
Huntingdon Life Sciences 110
Hutchings, Greg 44

i2 42
IBM 102, 111
IMS Health 62

In Search of Excellence (Peters &
    Waterman) 52–3, 55
Income Data Services 40
industrial relations 26–8
information
    data processing age 96–7
    overload 100
    Porter's five box scheme 104
    technological ability 96
    timely/accurate 95–6
    value of 105–6
Information Communication
    Technology (ICT) 97
Information Resource Management
    (IRM) 103–4
information technology (IT) 9
    desktop delusion 100–1
    evaluation of projects 101
    learning cost 99–100, 103
    new economy 122
    problems 94–5
    productivity paradox 98–100
    vendorization of investment
        decisions 101–2
InterX 42
investment
    ethical 113
    risk management 91–2
    vendorization of decisions 101–2
    virtuous 111
Iowa Electronic Market (IEM) 86–7
ITV 34
ITV Digital 36–7, 76–7

Jaguar 55–6
Japan 53
Johnson, Paul 4
joint ventures 73–4

Keynes, John Maynard 3
Klein, Naomi 66

Lazards 18–19, 22, 34, 46
Lehman Brothers 64

Leyden, 121, 122
Linux 102
Lipitor 64
London Aquarium 108–9
Luter, Joseph 88–9
LVMH 29

McDonald's 56–8, 112
McKinsey consultants 32, 39, 41, 50, 55, 72, 73, 74, 79, 102, 127
management
    authority 53–4, 58
    control 31–3
    hiring back 57
    investor power 30–1
    relationship with investors 26–35
Manwaring, Tony 65
Marchand, Donald 105
Marconi 11–12, 28, 36, 43–4
Marine Stewardship Council 108, 109
market research 84–5
marketing 69–70
Markowitz, Harry 91–2
Marks & Spencer 28, 48, 49, 50, 52, 55, 92
Marx, Karl 29
Massachusetts Institute of Technology (MIT) 52
Matsushita 53
Maxwell, Robert 22
May, John 11
Mayo, John 36, 43–4
mergers and acquisitions 32–3, 72–5, 78, 122
Microsoft 51, 73, 98, 102, 121
Morgan, J.P. 29
MORI 85, 87
motivation 8
    associated with performance 50–1
    doubting consensus view 55–6
    financial 51–2
    happy workforce 52–3
    less managerial authority 53–4
    reversing the trend 56–8
Motley Fool 14

Motorola 53
Murdoch, Rupert 37, 76

Nabisco 41
Nadjarian, Fred 60, 63
NASDAQ 123, 128
Nash, John 87
Nasser, Jack 43
National Institute of Economic and Social Research 124
Nicol, Jim 44, 45
Nissan 78
Novo Nordisk 113

OECD 95, 97
ONdigital see ITV Digital
Oracle 42, 98, 101
Orme, Simon 94
owner-operators 18–19
ownership 8
    competing interests 29–30
    realignment with control 34–5
    relationship with management 26–35
    structure 31, 34

pay 8, 25, 37–8, 40–1, 54
People and Connections (Shell publication) 82–3
PepsiCo 33, 76
personal computers (PCs) 100–1
Peters, Tom 6, 52–3, 56
pets.com 67–8
pharmaceutical companies 60–1, 62–4
Phillips, Bill 119
Photobition 33
Porter, Michael 27, 104
Portfolio Selection 91–2
Pravachol 63–4, 69
Prebble, Stuart 36–7, 77
prediction see futurology
Procter and Gamble 67
productivity 2, 8, 9, 10, 116–17
    applied 21–2
    division of labour 19–21
    efficient management 57

importance 18–19, 22–3
IT spending 100–1
and motivation 49–58
understanding 22
profit 11
    at Amazon.com 77
    before and after tax 14
    declared 15
    measured 16
Prudential plc 25, 41

Quaker Oats 33, 41

recession
    as accidental 120
    corporate self-mutilation 125–6
    failure as normal 126–8
    over-reaction to 119–20, 123–4
    panic over 124–5
    as preventable 120–1
Renault 78–9
Republic of Ireland 16
resources 9, 114
risk insurance 109–10
risk investment 91–2
Roche 60, 63
Rothschild, Nathan 95, 105
Royal Dutch/Shell 82, 84, 92
    future scenarios 82–3, 86
RyanAir 127

S&P Index 75
Safeway supermarket 85
sales 69–70
Schering-Plough 63
Schwartz, Peter 121, 122
Securities Exchange Commission
    (SEC) 111
shareholders
    attitude toward M&A 73
    government legislation 28–9
    interests of 27–8
    as investors 29–30
    paying attention to 25
    power 30–1

return 41, 45
    value 30, 113
shortcuts 9
    buy your competitors 71–5
    form an alliance 78–80
    pay customers to do business with
        you 75–8
Siebel 99
Siemens 90, 112
Sky 36, 37
Smith, Adam 3, 20, 29–30, 52
Smithfield 88–9
SmithKline Beecham 67
social accounting 112, 113–15, 116
Solow, Robert 98
Southwest airlines 127
spin-offs 31–2, 34
stakeholders 26–8
Stanford Law School 14
start-ups 31, 128
stock markets 123–4
strategic management 27
Sun Microsystems 101, 102
sustainability agenda 111–13, 115–17
Swissair 127
Synott, William 103–4

talent
    aligned to business virtue 46
    contest 38–9
    demand/supply 40–1
    market churn 42–5
    market forces 37–8
    market price 39–40
    quality 41–2
    share options 45–6
Taubman, Alfred 22–3
Taylor, Frederick W. 21
telecommunications industry 89–90
Tesco 55, 85
Tocqueville, A. de 29
Tomkins 44
transaction theory 20–1
Triple Bottom Line 112–15
Trump, Donald 13

Unilever 109

vendorization 101–2
venture capital 30, 31
Verizon 68
vice/virtue tests
    boom/recession 129–30
    information technology 106–7
    management/shareholder
      relationship 35
    motivation 59
    need for management 59
    productivity 23–4
    shortcuts 80–1
    social, environmental, ethical
      117–18
    talent 47
Vodafone 45, 90

Von Neumann 88

Wal-Mart 49, 96
Walton, Sam 96
Wasserstein, Bruce 18–19, 22, 34, 46
Waterloo, Battle of 95, 105
Waterman, Robert H. 52–3, 56
Watts, Philip 82, 83
Web services 101–2
Weber, Steven 121, 122
Wharton (Pennsylvania) 4
Wilson, Edmund O. 117
Wired magazine 121–2
Worcester, Bob 87
WorldCom 11, 15, 71, 74, 90

Zara 91, 92
Zenith OptiMedia 61

Printed and bound by CPI Group (UK) Ltd, Croydon, CR0 4YY

13/04/2025

14656568-0002